M000191048

From the
FARM
to the
HIGH SEAS

DEL STRODE

abbott press®

A DIVISION OF WRITER'S DIGEST

Copyright © 2014 Del Strode.

All rights reserved. No part of this book may be used or reproduced by any means, graphic, electronic, or mechanical, including photocopying, recording, taping or by any information storage retrieval system without the written permission of the publisher except in the case of brief quotations embodied in critical articles and reviews.

Abbott Press books may be ordered through booksellers or by contacting:

Abbott Press
1663 Liberty Drive
Bloomington, IN 47403
www.abbottpress.com
Phone: 1-866-697-5310

Because of the dynamic nature of the Internet, any web addresses or links contained in this book may have changed since publication and may no longer be valid. The views expressed in this work are solely those of the author and do not necessarily reflect the views of the publisher, and the publisher hereby disclaims any responsibility for them.

Any people depicted in stock imagery provided by Thinkstock are models, and such images are being used for illustrative purposes only.
Certain stock imagery © Thinkstock.

ISBN: 978-1-4582-1646-5 (sc)
ISBN: 978-1-4582-1647-2 (e)

Library of Congress Control Number: 2014909685

Printed in the United States of America.

Abbott Press rev. date: 6/17/2014

Most of the salvage work and other tasks are from memory, so the methods and procedures to accomplish may be recorded slightly different. All the locations, dates, duty stations, and awards are from records. Some of the names of personnel listed have been changed to prevent possible embarrassment.

I would like to thank my wife of twenty-eight years for her support without which I could not have written this and without her assistance and understanding, I could not have finished.

I would also like to thank the Commanding Officers who had enough trust in me to assign responsibilities beyond that of my pay grade. I would also like to thank those who thought I was worthy enough to recommend and encouraged me to seek a commission. Although my career plans never included a commission, I am honored by those who thought I would better serve my country and myself as a commissioned officer.

It is to my three children and five grandchildren I dedicate this book

Whatever a sailor does in whatever uniform he wears, his family is the most important asset whether at sea or in port. I never fully realized that fact until several years later.

I was married at age nineteen to the piano player at the Taylor Road Baptist Church; Glenda McRary who was twenty years old; the year was 1957.

I was just beginning my Naval Career as a Third Class Petty Officer and Glenda stayed with me for the next 18 years and beyond although only God knows how.

I would be at sea much of the time leaving Glenda the responsibility of maintaining our home, managing the finances, and most important, raising the girls which she did a fantastic job. I was not much help even when the ship was in port and I could have been. I seemed to have a problem being a husband, a father and a sailor all at the same time. I cringe when I think about the stunts I pulled on her and the kids. I am saddened to think about what I missed with my family by taking fifty years to grow up. The only good I can say about my actions during those twenty-one years of marriage; I was a good provider. I would work a part time job nights and weekends whenever possible unless it interfered with a class. We lived in our first home purchased when I was a Second Class Petty Officer not yet twenty-one.

We had three daughters, Kim, Kris and Kelly all three are very bright girls. Kim is the oldest, and has a Doctorate in Engineering and has recently retired from NASA. Kris has a degree in Computer Science and works at Lockheed Martin as the Director of Software Engineering. Her husband Mark is an engineer and also works at Lockheed Martin. Kelly is the youngest, employed by the same large motel in Norfolk for over twenty years, and is currently the Controller. Kris and Mark have one daughter Lindsay presently in the eleventh grade and looking forward to college. Their two boys Connor and Chad are both in college and so is Kelly's oldest daughter Jordan. Kelly has another daughter, Taylor who is in grade school.

We made it possible for the girls to get an education and they took advantage of the opportunity. Their initiative and motivation accomplished their goal of a higher education.

Glenda and I separated in 1978 and divorced while I was working in Cuba. I remarried for all the wrong reasons in 1981 to Carol Weston while still in Cuba. It was not a happy marriage and did not set well with my daughters.

She passed away in 1984 losing her battle against cancer at age forty-two.

I married my present wife Lillian Nicholas in 1986 in Duval County Florida where I moved after retiring. Through her love and kindness, she has succeeded in bringing the kids and me closer. They have accepted her as my wife and their stepmother showing her their admiration and respect. They were unable to do that with my last wife.

This book is an autobiography about a sailor, his working career, before, during and after serving in the U.S. Navy.

I decided early on I was going to be a "lifer" and earn a retirement from the Navy. Not long after making that decision, I knew I did not want to be an officer. I would follow the teaching, if not the work ethics, of those who were quick with advice to "get all you can and run like hell".

I served on two aircraft carriers, three repair ships, two salvage ships and three shore stations during my twenty years and twenty days of service in the U.S. Navy. I was a deep-sea diver and assigned to duty stations to serve as a diver ten out of the eleven years I maintained the diving qualifications. I have served in pay grades E1 through E9, with several specialties, including a number of collateral duties. Diving and salvage as both second and first class was one of those specialties but unlike most divers, I do not consider it the most important.

I attended school and was certified in Non Destructive Testing procedures obtaining a license to handle isotopes of radioactive materials. I attended two welding schools, certified and worked as a high-pressure welder on twelve-hundred pound steam systems. I attended school for ship handling, underway Officer of the Deck and Command Duty Officer in port. I was an accomplished ship handler with advanced seamanship skills and with hands-on training in navigation prior to satellites. I received certification in advanced firefighting and shipboard damage control procedures after attending several schools. I have served as the damage control assistant (DCA), chief master-at-arms (CMAA), command senior enlisted advisor and as a division officer at three different commands. I volunteered and served in positions in addition to underway OOD that were normally filled by Officers.

I paid a visit to the Army Recruiter in Portsmouth to discuss the possibility of leaving the Navy at the end of my ten years of service and volunteering for helicopter flight training. The Recruiter established that I was eligible but I changed my mind and reenlisted for six more years. I would be advancing to Chief Petty Officer and that changed my mind about the Army. I also volunteered for Swift Boat duty in Viet Nam but the Navy disapproved my request because I was the wrong rating.

I finished my twenty-years and twenty days and left the Navy with a retainer at age thirty-seven.

After the Navy, I was a real estate salesperson, appraiser, broker and owner of a real estate firm. I also owned and operated a welding business prior to leaving the Navy. I held a position in the local Norfolk Naval Shipyard in the Progress Section assigned as project manager and ship superintendent for repairs. I worked for the Department of the Navy overseas as the head of two branches of a ship repair facility, the dry docking officer and weight test director. I later took the superintendent position of a large public works facility. I exercised return rights just short of five years overseas back to the same desk at the shipyard in Portsmouth due to family illness. I retired to Florida at age forty-seven after losing my wife to cancer.

I left retirement for eighteen months to establish a computerized facilities management program at the local Naval Base. I volunteered to act as the Public Works Superintendent to assume the duties of the defunct O&M contractor at Mayport Naval Station and assisted in awarding a new contract.

Although I did not have any formal recognition for my educational efforts, I did complete several correspondence courses in my pipe fitter rating and many others in a variety of professional subjects. I also spent many hours in college level classes and lectures mostly in Industrial Engineering. These classes, and on the job training especially in supervisory skills prepared me for early promotions and to serve in several officer positions. As a civilian, I served in a few positions normally assigned to engineers.

I was born in 1938 in a small wood framed house located in a valley surrounded by grassy pastures blending into tall hard wood trees. Our home was located on a dirt road several miles from Tompkinsville Kentucky with my Grandparents as our closest neighbor. I can remember loading the horse drawn wagon with our family and grandparents with every one seated in straight back chairs and traveling that dirt road to town. I also remember sitting on a wooden bench with dad and grandpa in front of the court house while the women did their shopping. We watched two men, one at each end of a board walk across the street having a gunfight. This part of the State was wild and untamed even for 1942 and shootings were not uncommon. In fact, the doctor who delivered me shot a man seated next to his wife in a restaurant in Tompkinsville soon after we moved to Illinois.

I had a brother four years older than me and another brother who is now deceased. My Dad worked for the WPA to support the family and my mother was skilled at doing the most with the least. They too are now deceased. Dad moved the family to Illinois in 1942 in search of work. Life was not easy, my family moved frequently from one farm to the other. Sometimes we lived in town but mostly on a farm. Dad worked as a hired hand and we lived on the farm when the farmer had a house for us. Relocating created a hardship for the family and especially for me having to adapt to different schools and making new friends. It did teach me to take care of myself and to handle the school bully who would inevitably test me and we would end up in a fistfight after school. We would usually be friends after that but if not he would at least leave me alone. My sensitivity to the least amount of hostility directed at me continued to provoke physical confrontations that often landed me in trouble.

I can remember the first train I ever saw, my first bike that I would ride around the small town and was so proud to own. I had my first dog while living in that same small town. He would walk to school with me and meet me when school let out. A solid black Cocker Spaniel with big eyes and a sad look even when his tail was wagging, I named him Sad Sack. He was a spirited little fellow and always by my side, going with me wherever I went. He was also my first tragedy in life, he went blind and my older brother took him into a nearby cornfield and shot him, I cried on and off for weeks.

Ms. West was the Teacher - I am in the front on the right.

I attended one-room country schools, two as I remember. In these schools, one teacher taught grades one through eight. I also attended the larger consolidated schools with rooms for each grade and a teacher for each subject. What I learned in my brief nine grades of formal education served me well in the following years. I was a straight A student although I never took a book home except for a book report but I dropped out after the ninth grade. I would have liked to finish high school and gone on to college but it was not possible under the circumstances. I did get a high school diploma the second year I was in the Navy. The diploma was from the same school I would have graduated from had I continued. Dad's wages were not the best so I felt I should help out. I was working on the farm at age twelve when not in school. I drove farm equipment, hauled grain to the elevator and I worked alongside grownups by the time I was fourteen.

When I turned fifteen, I was out of school so I wanted a full time job but we lived in the country several miles from town. Since I did not have transportation, I took a room near the bottling company in Urbana where I found employment as a labeling machine operator. I soon saved enough money to purchase a car and move back home. I took and passed the driver's license test as soon as I turned fifteen as kids in Illinois could at that time.

I quit the bottle labeling job and I started a winter time job setting pins in a ten-pin bowling alley at night and weekends. I was driving home after work late one night during a snowstorm. The road had disappeared caused by the blowing snow and I ended up in the ditch forcing me to walk home. I retrieved my car the next day and the interior was full of snow from a small crack in the back window. I used a tractor to tow it to the barn and commenced drying it out.

It was at the bowling alley I met a couple men who worked for the federal government on a team surveying roads. They informed me of an opening and they thought I should apply. I did and got the job in the dead of winter and damn near froze before spring. I learned the two men had served and recently been discharged from the Navy. After I heard a few sea stories, I decided I was going to join because it sounded like a great way to get out of town. Besides, where else could I get free-living quarters, clothing, three squares a day and vacations all over the world with free travel. In addition, I would be paid twice a month, in cash and best of all it provided a career in an honorable profession.

I turned seventeen in April 1955 and was on my way to the Navy recruiter's office in Champaign Illinois before the week was out. The person behind the desk invited me to have a seat and as soon as I sat down, started asking me a barrage of questions. Although back then a high school education was not necessary to enlist, he seemed disappointed that I did not have a diploma. It was commonplace for a judge to give a young man who found himself on the wrong side of the law a choice, join the service or go to jail. I considered myself a good prospect because at least I had a clean record. Next I was given a test which I am sure was to establish that I was not a complete idiot by the simplicity of the questions. I had to take an approval form to my parents to sign granting permission that would not have been necessary had I been eighteen. The recruiter shook my hand, dismissed me and requested I return in a week. Meantime I told my best friend Jim Kesterson who was a year older than I and had quit school after finishing the eleventh grade. He thought it was a great idea so he rushed into town to see the same recruiter. We returned at the end of the week to find we were scheduled for a physical at the Air Force base in Rantoul. After all requirements were completed, including the swearing in, we were on our way to the Great Lakes Naval Training center in late May. The beginning of all enlisted Military Careers or service of any duration starts in Boot Camp.

The first priorities were unbelievable haircuts which we would not need another for at least a year. Next, we had dental exams, uniforms issued, and then given a battery of tests. We had no clue of the purpose or importance of these tests. We were assigned to the same Company that had a Petty Officer First Class with a Quarter Master Rating as the Company Commander. He was probably a nice person, but if he was, he did a good job of hiding it. I never saw anyone get so mad when we failed to respond to him with sir. Chief Petty Officers and First Class were the only ones used for that purpose and schooled in the art of training recruits.

I am not sure about now but in 1955, we drilled in formation in all sorts of weather. We fell into formation and marched to and from all necessary movement about the training center grounds including meals. Our physical training was very similar to that of the other branches of the armed service. The obstacle course was a grueling test of one's ability and condition. The course proved to be too difficult for some but not for those of us raised on the farm. We did our laundry by hand in the washroom and hung it to dry in a room designed for that purpose. To hang clothing with small pieces of cotton twine referred to as small stuff required practice in order to do it correctly. However, we had incentives to do it correctly because, as an example, articles of clothing hung with anything but a square knot ended up on the floor. If the Company Commander had thrown it on the floor, he would usually walk on it, making it a chore to scrub clean. Some less important detail might get by the inspector's eye but never the granny knot. The drying room was also used to settle disputes among the recruits. I had an occasion to use it for that purpose once. I had to convince the asshole marching behind me to stop stepping on my heels.

Another custom that was unofficially encouraged and considered necessary for enforcing boot camp's rigid personal hygiene standards was known as the GI shower. If an individual in our Company did not take showers as often as necessary, it was up to us to give him one. Several of us would take part, using lots of soap and a clean, stiff bristled brush designed for use on floors. One of those showers was usually enough to change the habits of even the hardest of hard heads. We had the opportunity to use this method of training only once.

There were times when both Jim and I had doubts about our choice to serve, the drilling in formation rain or shine and all those seemingly stupid things we had to do. We were required to salute anything that moved, call everyone mister and sir. We had to shower every day, put on clean clothing and spit shine our shoes and even our boots.

About half way through training, we were turned loose on the good citizens of Milwaukee in our dress white uniforms. The city known for its beer turned out to have more available than we could drink but the fair city was short on girls, a luxury we had been without much too long.

Things seemed to get better after the Cinderella liberty, called that because it ended at midnight. Maybe we realized that there was a reason for all those silly things we were forced to do or perhaps we were just getting accustomed to it all. Whatever the reason, things seemed to get easier the last half of our training. Time passed quickly and before long, we were on the drill field in formation. We were joined by several other Companies ready to pass in review. The big wheels were seated in the grand stand and behind them on each side were the bleachers for guest seating. Many parents attended the graduation ceremony but neither Jim's nor my parents could make it.

Jim and I departed boot camp leaving behind more than a few friends and on the train back to Champaign for a much needed two-week leave period. I attended a few parties and other social events which provided girls of our age and some a bit older. Most of them were accustomed to seeing men in Air Force uniforms. I guess the different uniform might have had something to do with their eagerness to check us out. Check us out they did, a different one every night we were not hanging out with friends.

Our leave ended too soon and we had to head out to comply with our orders to the duty stations we had been assigned. Some of the men in our Company who had finished high school before joining were assigned schools but I was assigned to an aircraft carrier and Jim to shore duty in Beeville Texas. I was surprised he received orders to a shore establishment but I learned later why. One of the tests we took had much to do with assignments we were eligible for including schools. Later when reduced manning in the Navy was required, the test would be used to decide who would be given an early discharge. It was among the battery of tests we took in boot camp without knowing the importance or the ramifications of a low score. I learned later that I did not get a very high score on mine either, so I requested to retake the test and I improved it to an above average score. I qualified for several schools after serving enough time to prove I was deserving of them.

The first adventure in the Navy had begun and was the beginning of what would continue for the next twenty years.

The train ride to Norfolk was long but there were others in uniform. Some were older and more experienced at wearing the Navy uniform and interesting to talk with and help pass the time. The conductor was an elderly black gentleman with a fatherly attitude who would announce the States we were entering where alcohol could not be consumed by anyone under twenty-one. When we arrived at the station in Norfolk, there was myself and one other boot camp graduate who the old man had kept an eye on for the entire trip. He gave us his last warning "now you boys are going through a place like none other in the world, stay together and hurry on through East Main Street, don't stop for anything". He certainly was correct, I had never seen so many bars, pool halls and even a burlesque theater, all with flashing signs and most with hawkers at the door. I walked as fast as I could with a sea bag on my shoulder, which probably weighed as much as I did. It was getting late and since there was a YMCA nearby, I decided to spend the night and take a cab to the base the next morning.

The ship was at sea so I was required to check into the receiving station of the Norfolk Operations Base to await its arrival. Those of us who were unfortunate enough to use this facility will never forget the daily working party assignments. I scrubbed many walls, cleaned floors and unloaded many trucks. That experience ended in late 1955 when the ship arrived and moored at pier twelve, a pier built just for the larger ships. There was another sailor who was also waiting on the ship so we took advantage of base transportation and headed for pier twelve. The pier was wide and long and I was surprised at the size of the ship. As we walked down the pier, we saw sailors in work uniforms lying in nets and painting the side of the ship. I learned later that those sailors were nicknamed deck apes and they were using cargo nets that allowed access to the overhangs and sides to scrub, or chip and paint. It was apparent how those sailors came by their nicknames. The nylon nets designed for transporting cargo and supplies from the pier or supply ships when taking on supplies at sea. We reached the gangway, sat our sea bags down and stared at the monstrous vessel that was to be our home for who knows how long. Our apprehension about climbing that gangway to the Quarterdeck must have been apparent because along came a petty officer, a salty looking fellow with a tanned wrinkled face. He spoke with authority when he yelled to us "grab those damned bags and get your stinking ass up the gangway". He was on the pier supervising the deck apes in the cargo nets when he saw us. He was a Boatswain Mate Second Class who wore three hash marks, each providing proof of four years' service when I saw him again in a dress uniform.

USS Ticonderoga CVA 14

She was commissioned in 1944 and saw action in the Pacific earning five battle stars. She was decommissioned at the end of World War II and re-commissioned in 1950. The carrier had a straight flight deck and an open bow, as all aircraft carriers of that era. Although much smaller than the super carriers that followed a few years later, these lightweights were very functional. This picture, taken in the Virginia Capes in September 1955, was my first time at sea but by no means my last.

We saluted the Junior Officer of the Deck, an old timer, a Chief with a sleeve filled with hash marks who directed us to the personnel office. There we were promptly checked in and assigned to the Administration Division for processing. While assigned to that division we would learn about our new home, her mission, and her vital statistics. Job assignments which would correspond with the manning requirements of the ship were the last functions of the Division.

The only classification I had been assigned was to the Engineering field as a Fireman Apprentice wearing two small red stripes on my left sleeve. I remembered the advice from the men on the survey crew to avoid the "black gang". This was the nickname for boiler tenders and machinist mates working in the engineering rooms in the days when coal fired the boilers. When asked what I had done before the Navy, I said I had done some plumbing work, which was not a complete lie. I helped a person fix a leak in his basement piping which took about an hour. Anyway, as a result I was designated a Pipe Fitter Striker (apprentice) where my workspace was located several decks above the engine rooms.

After the indoctrination was complete, I was assigned to the Repair (R) division and turned over to the leading Petty Officer, a First Class Pipe Fitter. He took me to their berthing compartment and assigned me a rack nobody wanted including me. It was the fourth up from the deck and located under a ventilation motor so close there was hardly enough room to turn over. This monster ran day and night and made a sound similar to a jet engine warming up. In order to sleep, I would press one ear into the pillow and my arm over the other. The first morning reveille was another rude awakening, literally. The word was passed over the one MC, which was the ships loudspeaker system, "all hands heave out and trice up, the smoking lamp is lit in all berthing spaces". The R Division's duty petty officer was going up and down each row of bunks yelling obscenities while beating on a trash container lid. Of course, not all duty petty officers used the same approach or terminology but it was still a rude way to wake each day. Failure to put the flameproof cover on your mattress and/or raising your bunks was sure to provide you with two hours extra duty after knock off ships work at 1600. The leading Petty Officer assigned most extra duty for violation of policies in the berthing compartment. The Master at Arms force usually assigned other violations of regulations that were not work related. If the infractions were of a more serious nature, you would be placed on report and taken to Captains Mast. We had a brig with a detachment of marines who guarded the prisoners among their other duties. I was surprised to learn how the smallest infraction of rules could cause a sailor to receive three days of piss and punk. Another term we hadn't learned in Boot Camp was for bread and water handed down from Captains Mast. The most common infraction that would land you in the brig was disrespect toward a superior Petty Officer or Officer. Although brig time was harsh punishment, it was authorized under the Uniformed Code of Military Justice (UCMJ) The Articles for the Government of the Navy better known as Rocks and Shoals Justice system which preceded the UMCJ was harsher and much less humane.

Turning in at night was at 2200 hours and was much easier to accept in tone although it was not quite like your mother tucking you in and kissing you good night. At 2000 hours, the word was passed "sweepers, sweepers, man your brooms, give her a clean sweep down fore to aft, empty all trash containers over the fantail". Again, instructions were passed over the ship's intercom system at precisely five minutes before Taps; we heard the word tattoo, tattoo. Then we heard; all hands turn into your own bunks, keep silence about the decks, the smoking lamp is out in all berthing spaces. This was followed by playing the short version of the song Taps after the evening Prayer. Of all the ships I served aboard for the next twenty years this routine remained unchanged, it was a custom and it served a distinct purpose.

The pipe shop was on the second deck, below the hanger deck and shared by the ship fitter and sheet metal shops. I remember three people very well, the Petty Officer Third Class who was my immediate supervisor, the Pipe Fitter leading First Class Petty Officer and the Chief Petty Officer. The Chief said very little to anyone and seemed to always be watching everything going on while standing with one foot on the peddle of the sheet metal sheer with a coffee mug in one hand.

The ship was divided and numbered into three sections from forward to aft as A, B, and C-sections and the decks below the hanger deck were numbered starting with two. The second deck was also known as the damage control deck. All decks above the hanger deck were numbered starting with one but preceded by a zero. The Pipe Fitters routine work consisted of head (bath rooms) checks daily to insure there were no fresh or salt-water leaks and all flushing devices were in good working order. Most of the shop personnel were divided into groups of two or three men, of which one was a Petty Officer in charge. Each group would be assigned a section of the ship using this numbering system. After the muster was complete each day, the teams would proceed to the heads located in their assigned area to check for any needed repairs. There was also a trouble call log where phone calls from those who wanted to report leaks or other problems requiring immediate attention. The shop supervisor would assign the appropriate personnel to investigate and make repairs if needed. The third method of work generation for

Pipe Fitters was by written job orders mostly from the engineering spaces. The watches I and the other non-rated stood were sounding and security that required checking voids and spaces throughout the ship from the second deck. This was accomplished by lowering a metal tape down the length of a pipe that reaches to the bottom of the void or space and checking for any dampness that would indicate flooding. The other watch was as a messenger in Damage Control Central where most engineering functions were monitored.

The Third Class Petty Officer I worked for on plumb check would always need some tool, which was not in his plumbing tool bag that I was required to carry. He would dispatch me to the shop to retrieve it and give me a limited amount of time to return. Of course, he would sit on his ass while he waited. On one such occasion, we were working on the 03 level four decks above the shop. I was busting my butt to get there and back with a tool he needed. The passageway hatches above the main deck are without doors and have raised combings about eighteen inches off the deck. I was running and literally jumping through the hatches when I collided with a two star Admiral. We both got up off the deck and I was visibly shaken, stammering and stuttering. After what seemed like an hour of him staring at me, he broke into laughter and told me to carry on but instructed me to go a little slower through hatches. This was not the best way to meet your first Admiral who I later learned was Commander Carrier Division Two.

The leading first class PO was a quiet type, very knowledgeable and a friendly person, easy to talk to and ask questions. The Chief was not to be questioned or even spoken to except to answer him. You could talk to God anytime but only through the first class PO could you talk to the Chief.

Rope yarn Sunday was a routine where the ship's crew was given every Wednesday afternoon off for the express purpose of mending, patching and attending to uniforms. When underway, Saturday was a work day but we had Sundays off except for the routine watches and could attend any of the available Church services. When in port, we continued Rope Yarn Wednesday and most Saturday mornings we held personnel uniform inspections. This was the routine and we rarely deviated from it except for an emergency or another ships function.

We departed Norfolk in route to the Mediterranean Sea not long after I reported for duty in the fall of 1955 and returned in August 1956.

The cruise was an experience. I went ashore as much as possible and the three months I worked as a mess cook was very interesting and educational as well.

There was a tragedy on the flight deck killing six sailors and the pilot. I am describing the events of this accident from memory because I could not find anything about it from researching the internet. A plane was coming in for a landing and it received a wave-off by the Landing Signal Officer. The abortion of a landing for various reasons was not uncommon. When the pilot attempted to gain elevation, his arresting gear hook caught the nylon safety barrier, a net rigged for stopping a plane if it fails to connect with the arresting cables. There were several men working on deck behind the barrier. All but six made it out of the plane's path although some of them were injured. The deceased were taken to the hanger deck for transporting to the chill boxes below decks. It was an unpleasant task so they detailed the mess cooks to do the job, since we were accustomed to performing unpleasant tasks such as cleaning up after a bunch of slobs. We got the job done but finding space in the chill boxes proved difficult and required moving food items around to make room. Most of the stretchers ended up on top of the bags of carrots. We were sworn to secrecy concerning the exact location of the bodies because specifics might not have been too good for the crew's appetite. I was assigned to the crew who started work early each morning to break out the days vegetables. We had one fellow on the team who was always late and missed the majority of the work. So on this; the first morning after placing the deceased in the boxes, we saved the carrots for him. He showed up late again and we were already taking the produce topside. The leader of the crew ordered him to break out a few bags of carrots while we waited and watched. He let out a scream and came out of there white as a ghost. The idiot had crawled between two stretchers and suddenly realized what they were. We all felt bad about the dirty trick we played on him, I know I did. However, it did improve the kid's work ethics and he was the first to show up for the morning break out from then on.

Shortly after returning from the long Mediterranean cruise, we were sent to the Norfolk Naval Shipyard for an overhaul that included a new angled flight deck and enclosed bow.

I was an old salt by then having spent a year onboard, most of that time at sea. I had done a little gambling during the long cruise and had amassed a nice sized nest egg.

I was assigned to help install deck drain piping from the flight deck to the fog foam firefighting stations on the second deck. Having to penetrate two decks rendered this a pipe fitting undertaking of sizable proportions. In late September, the Chief came down to the second deck where we were working and presented me with a choice. He said he had been informed two men were needed for transfer to the Naval Amphibious Base at Little Creek Va. He told me he believed in choosing the best workers and those who demonstrated the best aptitude and ability were the most deserving and that is why he chose me and the other sailor. I had heard this rationale from the Chief once before when I was assigned to the mess decks for

3 months only that time it was to do a good job serving my shipmates. I remembered this logic for the next 19 years and used it when it was necessary for me to choose personnel for special assignments or privileges.

Of course, we both accepted the opportunity for a change of scenery and the new experiences of being ashore but not subjected to the boot camp atmosphere.

I took a couple of weeks of shore leave returning home where I purchased 1953 red Mercury convertible and paid cash from my gambling money.

I departed the Ship in November 1956 and reported to the Amphibious Base the same month eager to see what shore duty was all about.

The US Naval Amphibious Base, Little Creek Virginia was homeport to twenty-seven ships and several resident commands including Explosive Ordnance Disposal Group Two, Construction Battalions, Seal Teams 2, 4, 8, 10 and later Harbor Clearance Unit Two are just a few. Over the next several years I would be stationed at some of these commands.

I checked into the Base and assigned to the Security Department. I was non-rated, a Fireman (pay grade E3) ready for Pipe Fitter Third Class (E4) and promoted a short time later. During the first year at Little Creek, I stood gate sentry watches as my primary duty and traffic control as a collateral duty. I received my first letter of commendation in the Navy for traffic control during the celebration of Navy Day at Rockwell Hall.

Having that great looking convertible turned out to be more expensive than I had anticipated and required I live on my good credit from payday to payday. There was a gas station where I would charge my gas, a young lady bar tender who would provide me with drinks on credit and sometimes even provide me sleeping quarters. On payday, I would make my rounds and settle my debts and start all over. This continued until I met with misfortune at the first red light I came to after leaving the watering hole where my friend worked. I failed to stop at the red light and rear ended another car and since I had the top down and no seat belt I was catapulted from the car. I regained consciousness in the sickbay at the nearby Amphibious Base. A State Policeman was waiting to ask me a few questions concerning drinking while driving. He informed me the ambulance personnel had pulled me out from under the car with a large gash above my left eye. I was fortunate not to have suffered damage to my vision and also without a ticket.

In May 1958, I was promoted to Second Class (E5) and assigned to the Master at Arms Force, Captain's Driver, courtroom orderly, brig runner and sometimes JOOD on gate one, all within the Security Department. The primary job of the Master at Arms force was to maintain order, enforce uniform regulations and attend Captains mast with sailors who were placed on report for violating the rules. The collateral duty as brig runner and courtroom orderly went together because the guilty usually had to be transported to the brig. We held several Special Court Marshals mostly from the ships home ported at Little Creek. The collateral duty of Captain's driver was very educational and was the easiest of all my duties. I was on call twenty-four hours a day but I seldom had to drive the CO after hours unless it was prearranged. On one occasion, the CO asked that I take his daughter downtown for a dental appointment because his wife was unable to drive her. That was the only time I transported a family member.

Of all the court marshals I attended, there was one I really felt sorry for the young man. He was found guilty of a crime and awarded a Bad Conduct Discharge. In such awards, I was required to take the convicted to Sears with a supply purchase order for clothing to replace their military uniform. The uniform he was wearing and all his other military clothing turned into the Lucky Bag. It was a stowage building used for that purpose and any other clothing found adrift or unclaimed in the barracks. After returning to the base with the new civilian, I stayed with him while the personnel office finished final processing. My standing orders required that I drive him to the main gate and literally boot him from the vehicle. I could not do that, instead I opened the door and wished the teary-eyed young man good luck when he returned home. I waited and watched until he reached Shore Drive and started hitch hiking toward town.

I made many brig runs for different reasons but there was one that stands out in my mind because it was so tragic. I went to the personnel office to pick up the orders and deliver a First Class Petty Officer from the Main Gate to the brig at Camp Allen. I had no idea what he had been accused of but I knew it had to be something very serious for a Petty Officer First Class to be incarcerated. When I returned to the base, I learned a base police officer had been checking out a suspicious car parked at a vacant building used for temporary quarters for Midshipmen when they were on the base for training. When he opened the door, he saw a man having sexual relations with an obviously underage girl. He attempted to apprehend the person who was in civilian clothing by grabbing him by the shirt but he managed to get to his car while the officer looked after the girl. The officer radioed the main gate to stop the car and they did, and notified the Command Duty Officer who arranged for my trip to the brig. The incident, as horrific as it was, got even worse. We learned it was the man's nine-year-old daughter he was having sex with which the officer witnessed. I made several trips back and forth from the brig taking him to see different shrinks, at the dispensary and the Naval Hospital in Portsmouth. On one such trip, he asked me to stop by his house so he could speak to his wife. I did not think he deserved any favors but I thought his wife probably needed to talk to him. I normally had a driver as I did this time and I carried a side arm. I had the driver go to his house and I instructed the prisoner to stay in my sight at all times while I gave him 10 minutes to talk with his wife. Everything went well and we were back heading for Camp Allen with a quiet and withdrawn prisoner. This man was not only a pedophile but also a sociopath who showed no remorse or guilt. He received a Bad Conduct discharge and booted from the Navy but I thought he got off too easy. There were several other life-altering events in addition to leaving home at age fifteen and serving on an aircraft carrier at seventeen. Experiencing the worst the human race has to offer will rush anyone into adulthood.

I had a visit from my old school friend, Jim. He was on his way home to Sidney, IL and stopped to see me on the way. I was directing traffic at the intersection of a four-lane road when I spotted him. After peak traffic hour was over and I was off work, we went to the barracks and had a long talk. He informed me he had been discharged after two years due to a low score on one of the tests we had taken in Boot Camp. He also told me he did not like the Navy. He made no effort to stay in and had only wanted to join because his dad was a Chief in the Navy during the war. I only saw Jim on one other occasion when I was home on leave when he was working on a residential roofing crew. I tried to look him up years later when he would have been sixty and I learned, he, along with his wife and entire family had moved to South Florida years before. His ex-wife informed me he was deceased as was his mother, father and younger brother. I asked her what he and his younger brother's had to die at such a young age but I never heard from her again.

I had another visitor, this time from a shipmate and friend Red Ruckels from the Ticonderoga. We had made a few speed runs on weekends to his home in Dayton, Ohio. We partied a little too hardy during that visit and I was driving him around the base while trying to sober him up. I lost control of his Oldsmobile on a curve, ran it into a deep ditch and turned it over. We were not injured but I cannot say the same about the car. Because I was in the Security Department, all the base police knew me and the old sergeant on duty liked me so he called a tow truck, paid to have the car towed off base and did not make a formal report of the accident. I paid him back for the tow the next day and he informed me he had spoken to the base duty officer and smoothed it over with him so that nobody else would be notified. This old guy was a real character; he would come into the guard shack on late night duty, have coffee and entertain us with his little dance routine. He would dance around while singing, "Ole Molly was working in the circus, she danced first on one leg and then the other and between the two she made her living". I was standing a midnight watch at Gate One when the old gent came through the gate to patrol a parking lot used by sailors who couldn't get on the base with their cars. We heard several rounds fired from the lot. We found out later, he caught a kid stealing hubcaps and when he did not stop running when told, the Sergeant started firing at him. He was lucky the boy got away because the old man would have surely gone to jail if he had killed or wounded the kid. I am sure of one thing, that kid will never steal hubcaps again. On another occasion while I was standing the JOOD watch on gate one the sentry stopped a Navy bus with one occupant. The sentry was a young sailor from West Virginia who ran moon shine for his Grandfather and was very much a hillbilly. When he went onboard the bus, the driver asked if he could get the drunken sailor to clean the vomit off the floor. Seaman Stamper, the sentry retrieved a mop and while I was watching, he had the sailor swab up his mess. With one quick movement, the drunken sailor who was a black man swung the mop and hit Stamper upside the head. I feared what was going to happen next so I hurried onto the bus to prevent a killing. By the time I got to him, he was trying to put a clip into his Colt 45. I was able to get the clip away from him but he hit the drunk upside the head with the gun. I removed Stamper from the bus, told the driver to get the sailor to his ship and sent Stamper to the barracks to clean up.

The base Captain (CO) was a bit eccentric when riding in his staff car, especially off base. Although it was illegal, he required me to use the stationary red light atop the car when I drove him anywhere off base. He also had a serious hang up about taking care of the grass on the base. If he saw anyone parked on it, he would require me to write up a report chit so they would go before him at

Captain's Mast. On one occasion, he requested that I stop alongside a car without a driver. I had to radio the base police to come ticket the car. When the police officer showed up, he skidded to a stop on the grass behind the car. The Captain jumped out and gave him hell for tearing up the grass. He was there to issue a ticket to the parked car for doing the same thing. He wanted to make improvements to the golf course grounds but could not get sufficient funds to accomplish the job. He went to the Sea Bees and directed them to do the work he wanted. It took several men, lots of equipment and turned into a major project. It became a problem when the wrong person got wind of what he was doing. As I understood it at the time, he was using government labor and equipment for something that required funding and accomplishing from non-appropriated sources and funds. Captain Smith was relieved and transferred soon afterwards.

I enjoyed my first tour of shore duty because my job provided an opportunity to see the worst and the best of the sailors who served. I was able to see the mixtures of personalities and the life styles of young men from all over the country. It was an education and combined with the responsibilities of my varied assignments made those two years an exciting time.

Two more life-altering events happened during my tour of shore duty. I was married at age nineteen and I re-enlisted for six more years. As a re-enlistment incentive,

I requested a six month Class C welding school in San Diego and then to a Battle Wagon for duty. I received orders to the school and for further transfer (FFT) to the USS Independence CVA 62. I had to fly to California so I knew I would need a car and I started looking as soon as I could. I found a 1948 Studebaker Champion, which was in good running condition even if it did use more oil than gas. The guy who sold it to me was a used car salesman and a retired Chief and after hearing my situation he told me if I didn't wreck the car he would buy it back from me when I transferred. I paid one hundred twenty five dollars for the car and he gave me the same amount back just before departing.

The school taught arc welding of mild steel with both cellulose and low hydrogen fluxed rods. There was some classroom work but most days were spent in the welding booth with the close guidance of an experienced welder. We also had instructions in oxy-acetylene welding of ferrous metals, brass welding and silver brazing. It was hot, dirty and very strenuous with few breaks but the training was required for anyone who wanted to be proficient as a pipe fitter.

USS Independence CVA 62

USS Independence CVA 62 built in the Brooklyn Navy Yard and commissioned in January 1959 a Forestall Class Carrier. She was decommissioned September 1998 after serving 39 years on the high seas.

During acceptance trials, she recorded her first arrested landing when a TF-1 Trader trapped aboard March 2, 1959.

A short time after arriving at her homeport in Norfolk she headed for the Naval Base Guantanamo Bay, Cuba for ten weeks training by the Fleet Training Group. During that training period, she conducted carrier suitability tests for the new F4H-1 Phantom II.

The Navy flew me to Guantanamo Bay to catch the ship in December 1959. Carriers do not spend a lot of time in port especially when displaying the air power that was so important during the cold war. The Indy was taking water onboard when I arrived in Gitmo. The evaporators, which turn seawater into potable water, could not keep up with the demand due to the omission of the installation of some required machinery.

The gates at Gitmo were permanently closed, restricting liberty to the base using the various clubs, bowling alley, golf course and the beaches. We were anchored out and had to take liberty launches to the fleet landing. The base provided transportation to and from the clubs in what were commonly known as cattle cars. The large trailers resembled a rig you would see on the highway for transporting cattle, but these had seats installed. I'll never forget the experienced of riding in this rig with a bunch of sailors after some heavy drinking. In those days, the drinking habits of the average sailor differ from the modern sailor. The theme, work hard and play hard referred to drinking and raising hell ashore but still getting the job done onboard.

The ship had eight twelve hundred pound boilers, two each located in four main machinery spaces and four evaporators located in two auxiliary machinery spaces. The piping system that supported the boilers was from a mixture of the alloys, carbon, chromium and molybdenum. The piping had to withstand the twelve hundred pound steam and over nine hundred degree temperatures from the eight boilers. Because of the serious consequences to personnel from a high-pressure leak, only qualified personnel were permitted to make repairs to the piping system. There was only one welder on board who was permitted to weld on the high-pressure piping and he was not trained or certified. When the ship returned to Norfolk, I requested and received orders to the HP arc welding training and certification class at the Norfolk Naval Shipyard. The course took four weeks and consisted of training in the identification and welding of the high pressure piping systems containing alloys not found in any other system. I spent several hours each day practice welding two six-inch pipes together. Each joint prepared with a sixty degree included bevel and tack welded together. The joint would have a chill ring backing leaving an eighth inch root opening. The welding test consisted of piping placed in a corner and required welding in the horizontal and another in the vertical position with only six inches of clearance on two sides. To finish welding the opening closed took several passes and could not have any undercut on either pipe. The final two welded samples were x-rayed and allowed a minimum number of flaws for certification. It was not uncommon for some workers in training not to get a sample welded good enough to send for testing. A shipyard worker in the booth next to mine just could not weld the blind side of the pipe and was finally sent back to his shop. I had six months of extensive training in the art of welding with all kinds of rods, on steel plates machined and the joint prepared exactly like the pipe joints. The plates were placed in the exact positions as the pipe. It was still difficult welding due to the closeness to the bulkhead on two sides.

In August 1960, we departed for our maiden cruise to the Mediterranean to join the other units of the Sixth Fleet

We were required to enter Mayport Naval Station and load the gear for the support of the fighter jets that would fly onboard soon after we departed. Since we would be in port over the weekend another fellow in the shop who had been stationed at the reserve fleet in Green Cove Springs invited me to join him to visit some friends. The family he knew were very nice and invited us to spend the weekend and they would take us back to the ship Sunday evening. My friend, another Second Class who also liked his beer, drank all he had and went to buy more Sunday morning. The young lady informed him the Blue Law prevented the sale of alcohol on Sunday. Vanlandingham acted as though he was going to cry, so the girl said hell sailor, don't cry I'll sell you a case. We were being taken to the ship Sunday night as promised, however, the Marines on the gate would not allow the car onto the base without a sticker. It's a long walk from the old gate off Seminole Road to the carrier berth. As luck would have it there was a staff car parked in the driveway of the house just inside the gate with the keys in the ignition. We jumped in, drove to the ship, parked at the head of the pier, jumped out and quickly boarded the ship in case the base police had been notified.

We steamed for approximately five days before reaching the Straits of Gibraltar which is the sea lane entering the Mediterranean Sea from the Atlantic Ocean. We visited several ports and spent many days at sea launching and retrieving aircraft while displaying our might. We made visual contact on and off with Russian submarines all throughout the cruise. It was as if they were following us and wanted us to know it. Training continued for the crew in the form of drills in distinguishing fires, nuclear, biological and chemical attacks (NBC) and other drills. All drills began with the sounding of General Quarters over the 1MC at all hours of the day and night. My GQ station was on the second deck at one of the many damage control lockers. The second deck is the damage control deck equipped with hydraulic valve boards that enable the fire main piping to be segregated into smaller loops to isolate damaged sections should it occur. There are other valve boards designed to pump water from compartments if flooding should happen from underwater damage.

I remember anchoring off the coast of Genoa, Italy and riding a liberty launch ashore. After departing the boat and climbing up a ramp to the street, we heard music coming from a bar on the other side. A friend and I crossed over to investigate the American sound and discovered a large sign with the name Elvis Presley. Neither of us had ever heard the entertainer sing before, but we heard him many times when we returned to our homeport. In those days, we had shipboard TV but it was closed circuit and only the newer ships even had that. We had a lot of mandatory training and movies most of the time to watch on the TV in our berthing compartment lounge. We were in high cotton with stationary bunks that did not require tricing up, no loud vent motors, and we even had air conditioning throughout the ship.

The best liberty on the cruise was going to Rome to attend the 1960 world Olympics and the opportunity to tour the ancient city. We anchored off the small port of Civitavecchia, Italy and took buses from the boat landing for the fifty-mile ride to Rome. Four of us from my shop ended up spending the first day at the games and then we rented a cab for the next day and toured the city of Rome. It was an exciting experience for a farm boy who grew up in Illinois and had never been any further from home than Indiana.

The cruise was uneventful with no major accidents other than a crash or two on the flight deck that was not uncommon considering the number of launches and landings per day and night.

I received a letter of commendation from the Captain for an emergency repair to one of the Destroyers serving as our plane guard during flight ops. The USS Cecil DD-835 had a main propulsion boiler taken out of service due to safety concerns. One of her boilers developed a leak on one of the tubes entering the mud drum. With the one boiler out of commission, the Destroyer could not keep up with the Indy during flight quarters, which made the repair an emergency. I spent several hours grinding and welding to complete the repair with the help of another pipe fitter. We had a Chief in charge of the pipe shop and he went with us so he could share in the letter we received. I assume this was his reason for going with us; he sure as hell was not any help. We were notified when the ship returned home that our emergency welding repair was inspected, tested and approved by the shipyard.

We had several valves that needed replacing but we had to make welding repairs to the valve bodies. The supply department did not have any spares onboard, a situation we rectified when we returned to the States.

We returned to Norfolk in March 1961 and spent the next five months in and out of port conducting carrier qualifications for pilots launching, landings, and other training preparing for the next deployment. It seemed everything we did was in preparation for the next deployment.

During this period, we purchased HP valves, piping and welding supplies in large quantities that we determined were required based on our first cruise. We had not yet experienced the requirement for flanges to be repaired or replaced because the system had not been in service long enough to have developed steam cuts. The maintenance of the relatively new twelve hundred pound steam main propulsion system was a learning experience for us all.

In August 1961, the Indy once again set sail for the Mediterranean for her second deployment joining units of the Sixth Fleet. We had to depart sooner than expected because of increased worldwide tension over the construction of the Berlin Wall.

I had an incident on liberty and was placed on report by the Shore Patrol. I got into a fight with a Marine Sergeant who was with one of our Air Squadrons. My Division Officer and Chief Engineer went with me to the XO screening and attempted to convince him I walked on water. It helped some because he dismissed me until he had a chance to further review my case. A few days later the three of us went in front of the XO again and this time I was referred to Captains Mast. He explained that the Sixth Fleet Admiral required violations ashore from anyone under his Command would have the corrective action taken reported in writing to him by the violator's Commanding Officer. Because by then I was a First Class Petty Office and my infraction was unbecoming of my pay grade, the Captain busted me to Second Class but suspended the reduction for six months. This meant I would have to keep out of trouble for that period of time or the reduction in rate would be executed. Although I was not, by any measure an angel that was the only time in my twenty year career I had to go to Captain's Mast except when I escorted another sailor.

During this cruise I spent much of my working days in the main propulsion machinery rooms cutting out and replacing one half up to one inch high pressure valves and removing, repairing and re-installing flanges that had suffered damage from steam cuts. Soon after being advanced to Petty Officer First Class I was required to take charge of the thirty three man pipe shop because the Chief had been transferred without a relief.

The most important requirement of a supervisor is his leadership ability but it also requires he have sufficient knowledge of the pipe fitter trade to teach and guide those of lower grades. I spent a lot of time in training manuals and correspondence courses to insure I had the necessary knowledge for training when required. We had a system in place in those days to determine if a man was ready to be recommended for the test for advancement called Practical Factors. Unlike some, I took the process very serious because it not only prepared the individual to take and pass the test it insured he could perform the duties. It was my responsibility to ensure all personnel of lower grades were able to demonstrate his level of knowledge and abilities to complete the Factors. A wide range of subjects in the pipe fitting, metal fabrication and damage control fields were included in the PFs. It was also my responsibility to teach them if they were deficient in any of those fields.

I remained in charge of the shop while continuing repair welding HP piping systems in the main machinery spaces although we had another qualified welder onboard. The Chief Engineer insisted I continue doing all the twelve hundred pound piping repair welding. I turned over all six hundred pound steam piping systems repair which supported the catapults and auxiliary machinery rooms to the Second Class Pipe Fitter. We returned to Norfolk from our second Med cruise in December 1961. We spent the next four months alongside the pier and on local Operations and training in the Virginia Capes before our next cruise in April 1962.

This would be my last Med deployment on the Indy and it required more replacement of valves and welding up steam cuts in flanges than the other two cruises combined. Many times I would be awakened in the middle of night to make welding repairs and I remember on at least one occasion I spent three straight days working in the number three main machinery space replacing steam valves and installing sections of piping. My two helpers would cut out valves, piping and flanges which required replacing or repairing. They had apparently heated and bent piping at ninety degrees instead of using fittings which weakened the pipe and caused steam blow-out.

We also had occasions when I worked all night cutting out flanges, resurfacing the face by welding the steam cuts, have them machined smooth for reinstallation. The supply officer got wind of our stock piling which we were not supposed to do. He came to the shop raising hell about it but the Chief Engineer settled him down. However, it was necessary to get the supply department in the loop by providing them with high and low amounts. We were able to do this now that we had experienced the actual requirements first hand and it was their job to order up to the high number and reorder when they reached the low number.

The Chief Engineer was a salty thirty-three year veteran and was a limited duty officer (LDO) Commander who was an expert on steam propulsion plants. He had a one hundred eighty degree curved brass piping device with a funnel on one end hanging above his desk in the Log Room. The name plate below the device declared it was a tool for blowing smoke up his ass but as far as I know, nobody ever tried to do that. He was a wise old bird with a good sense of humor and so senior in his rank that the Captain required him to take over the Executive Officer's duties when he went on leave. It is normal for the XO to be relieved by the Operations Officer also a Commander.

It was on this cruise he requested I, along with the First Class Machinery Repairman I worked with to come to his stateroom. He presented us each with Ensign Bars as a reward and his appreciation for our part in keeping all eight boilers on the line resulting in never missing a scheduled launching. He handed them to us and said for us to hang onto them and he would inform us when to put them on. Apparently, he had the necessary paper work completed and ready to submit, who knows, maybe he had connections in Washington because the other guy took the bars, but I respectfully declined. The Machinery Repairman was advanced to Ensign and transferred to another aircraft carrier a short time later.

My Division Officer, an LDO Lieutenant came into my shop visibly upset because his third request to retire in as many years had been disapproved. He blamed this disapproval on the Warrant Officer program being eliminated, creating an increase in demand in the LDO ranks. He was probably correct because I never saw more than two at any given time in the Warrant Officer's mess. This shortage might also have had something to do with our invitation to a commission. I had decided to make Master Chief when the E8 and E9 ratings were first established back in the late fifties.

The flight deck of an aircraft carrier is a very dangerous place, and although it is not recommended, we would go up to the "cat walk" which was a narrow walkway about four or five feet below the flight deck and watch the planes land. A Navy Photographer's Mate was holding his camera on the edge of the deck intending to take a picture of a jet coming in for a landing. The poor guy picked the wrong landing to photograph because it was a "hot" landing. The plane was coming in much too fast and when his tail hook caught the arresting gear cable it caused the plane to slam the deck hard enough to break off a wheel. That wheel came across the deck with such force it took the photographer's head off. There are accidents, some just as freakish as this one associated with landings and take offs but few from the cat walk. I recall another freak accident; a jet was attached to the catapult launching cable with the pilot preparing himself and his plane for launching but not yet ready. The word was out that the operator at the controls below the flight deck pushed the wrong button and catapulted him and his plane instead of the plane that was ready. This pilot never surfaced from the plane until it sank. It was determined he probably suffered physical disability from the jolt because he wasn't prepared.

We returned to homeport in August 1962 and remained in port for the next two months enjoying rest and recreation (R&R). In October, the Independence and other elements of the Atlantic Fleet rushed to the Caribbean to support quarantine operations against Cuba following the discovery of Soviet ballistic missiles on the island. All the weapon elevators were being used to deliver ordnance from the magazines. When the ordnance reached the flight deck, the aviation ordnance personnel loaded them onto aircraft. The work went on around the clock until all the many aircraft were armed with a variety of ordnance. The next day I went topside to view the armed aircraft and was amused to find "hello Castro" painted on the nose of some of the bombs. With stern warnings to Khrushchev during the one on one negotiation by phone between him and President Kennedy an agreement to remove all missiles was reached. With the crisis defused, we returned to Norfolk in late November 1962 where we conducted readiness exercises along the Eastern Seaboard. A short time later we entered the shipyard for an overhaul. During this yard period I left the Independence and was transferred to a much less arduous sea duty command. I had logged three Mediterranean cruises, two Caribbean cruises, and an unimaginable number of days at sea in the past three years and two months.

USS Vulcan AR 5

The AR5 was commissioned in June 1941 and decommissioned in September 1991 after 50 years of service to the Fleet. As shown in this picture we stayed very busy keeping ships of all types repaired. The exception was Destroyers which went alongside AD class tenders and Submarines used AS class for repair and scheduled availabilities. All the repair ships maintained two separate groups. The Repair Department personnel were assigned to the shops that serviced the ships requiring repairs and the Ships Company personnel who were assigned to take care of the needs of the ship.

I reported aboard the Vulcan in February 1963 and since I was a certified high pressure welder I was assigned to the welding shop located on the second deck at one end of the pipe shop. The shop was ideally located because almost all of our in-shop welding was performed from that shop. The leading Petty Officer of the shop was another First Class, who was not a very good welder. In fact he wasn't a very good Ship Fitter either, because he demonstrated very little knowledge of the trade. The pipe shop supervisor, George Doffner, a First Class Ship Fitter gave me a compliment not long after I came aboard. He requested I do all the welding on the pipe work for his shop because he didn't feel it necessary to hydrostatic test my welds before his men installed it onboard. George turned out to be a character with a strange sense of humor. He took emergency leave to attend his Mother's funeral and when he returned he was asked how it went. His reply was "it was a very simple ceremony. They just stuck a hambone up her butt and let the dogs drag her off. I am sure he intended that to be funny but it certainly was not. Another one of his supposedly funnies took place in the First Class mess. If we had grapes on the table he would skin one, stick it up his nose without being noticed, blow it out, and let it plop onto the table. George did have a reputation for being crude. When he was confronted about his strange ways he would say "what do you expect from a guy raised in a junk yard". His ambitions were as strange as his sense of humor because he looked forward to retiring and going home to operate the junk yard for his dad.

I found it strange at first that the senior First Class in the welding shop didn't do the shop welding. Another

First Class and I, with the help of two Second Class did all the welding on the ships alongside. The first time I saw a sample of his welding I knew why. It looked like dingle berries hanging from a dog's butt.

The Chief was a very likable young twenty five year old, Billy Richardson. Although he was a large man, he still had the appearance of being much younger. He and I were checking out a job order on a ship alongside one day when a young Ensign on the Quarter Deck stared at the Chief for a few seconds then asked his age. The Chief told him and the young officer, said, "damn and a Chief already". Billy asked his age and the officer replied twenty three and Billy responded "damn, and Ensign already". The Chief read about a small airport in Portsmouth which was offering a free indoctrination flight for the purpose of getting students interested in flight school. We got together one Saturday and took them up on the offer. After we landed, we stopped for a beer and the bartender served mine but he was carded, that's how young this Chief looked. Our paths crossed a couple times in the following years, once when he was a Warrant Officer and again when he was a LCDR after I had been out of the Navy for several years.

The US Navy in all of its wisdom deemed it necessary to change the hull group ratings several times during my active duty career. As a Third Class I was designated a fitter pipe (FP3), as a Second Class ship fitter pipe (SFP2), as a First Class ship fitter (SF1), as a Chief Petty Officer (SFC-A). The A was for acting, (I made permanent Chief when "acting" was discontinued), as a Senior Chief Damage Control (DCCS), and as a Master Chief Hull Technician (HTCM). The changes FP, SFP, SF, DC, and finally HT included Pipe Fitters, Metal Smiths, Carpenters /Damage Control personnel all with different trade experience and working in different shops. One of the expressions I heard from Pipe Fitters and Metal Smiths was "I would rather have a sister in a whore house than a brother a Damage Control man".

In those days repair ships did most of the work required on the ships they serviced which was beyond the scope of the ships personnel. On the Vulcan we did everything from simple repairs to ship alterations. One such shipalt, another First Class and I did most of the welding for the installation of a vertical replenishing deck on a supply ship. The ship was the USS Aldebaran AF10 that required a raised deck for helicopters to take off and land which would allow vertical replenishing of ships at sea. All of us who worked this job received letters of commendation, not only for the scope of work, but for getting the job completed as scheduled.

The Ship Fitters cut a large hole to remove and reinstall new laundry equipment on the deck below on a ship alongside. I no sooner had my equipment set up and started welding when the snow started coming down

49

which made it very difficult to see out of the darkened welding helmet. We rigged a lean-to which provided some relief from the blowing snow and enabled me to finish in time to allow the ship to get underway as scheduled.

A First Class in the pipe shop who was a salvage diver and another First Class in charge of the diving locker were instrumental in convincing me to request second class diving school. Since it paid hazard duty pay of fifty-five dollars a month, I thought I would give it a try. Looking back on what motivated me to become a diver, I would say it was the money because I never was gung-ho about diving. Once the request was approved, I was required to make an indoctrination dive in a deep-sea rig to test for claustrophobia, and a chamber run to sixty feet to test for 02 tolerance. Several treatment tables require breathing pure oxygen at that depth and some people are unable to tolerate the breathing media when under pressure. I witnessed one individual who had no idea he had claustrophobia until the Mark V helmet was placed on his head.

Diving school was a couple months duration but it was intense training and very physical. The school was held on the YFNB 17 which was an enclosed barge tied to a pier at the Naval Submarine and Destroyer Piers. I was transferred to the school for temporary additional duty (TAD) in October 1963. The barge was transferred to Little Creek Amphibious Base and commissioned as

Harbor Clearance Unit Two in 1966. It would later, 1982 I believe, be renamed Mobil Diving and Salvage Unit 2 but retained the same mission which was to provide diving and salvage operations wherever they were needed.

The senior instructor was a seasoned First Class Boatswain Mate, Leon Ryder, who started us on a five mile run at 0600 each morning. I swear that guy could run longer and faster backwards than most of us could run forward. BM1 Leon Ryder would in later years be referred to as Mr. salvage and retire after 30 plus years as a W4 Warrant Officer. After the run, we would have breakfast which was almost always good because the stew burner was a top notch Cook. Then we did thirty minutes of push-ups, jumping jacks, deep knee bends and "hello darlings". Of course when you were too tired to continue we suffered the name calling "you candy ass" and worse. Then we headed to the diving station located on the pier at the stern of the barge. It consisted of a wooden platform with a small enclosure housing the necessary diving equipment. We set up two hard hat diving rigs with stools to sit on while dressing two students. We were required to make about a ten minute bottom time dive in the silt and mud up to our neck. We continued making as many dives as possible during the day climbing a six rung steel ladder in and out of the water wearing the Mark V diving outfits which weighed in excess of two hundred pounds. It was surprising how many men were flunked out of school because they couldn't climb the ladder. A couple men who weighed over two hundred pounds were dropped from my class for that reason. It takes concentration and coordination to swing your feet from one rung to the other, strength alone is not enough. The barge was towed to deep water for our hard hat qualification dives. I made my required dives and on my last one I was seated on the dressing stool and as soon as my face plate was opened, I was informed Kennedy had been shot. My response was "it's about time someone shot the SOB" because I thought they were referring to Master Diver Kennedy who was stationed on the barge, not the President.

Those of us who survived the hard-hat (Mark V) training advanced on to training in open sea scuba diving after several days training in the Olympic size pool at the Naval Operating Base in Norfolk. One very unpleasant incident happened to me during the swimming endurance training while I was swimming the length of the pool and back wearing a heavy scuba weight belt. It was apparent I was having difficulty on the swim back but I made it and while I was holding onto the wall, catching my breath, the instructor pushed my head underwater with his foot. To this day, I'm not sure if he was attempting to drown me or to simply discourage me enough so that I would drop out. I didn't drop out. In fact, I graduated in the top ten percent of the class and returned to the Vulcan as a second class deep sea diver.

I learned a short time after completing the course that the Petty Officer Second Class who was my scuba swim partner in school was killed in Indian Head Maryland. He was diving in sixty feet of water and died of an embolism caused by holding his breath while coming to the surface. He was practicing buddy breathing from his swim buddy's mouth piece when he breathed water into his lung causing him to panic.

I returned to the welding shop and participated in diving tasks when needed while continuing welding as my primary duty. One of the first working dives I went on was to plug a sea suction on an aircraft carrier. The senior diver in charge of the diving locker was making the dive back under the ship when the air hose on his Jack Brown mask blew off. He gave the tender four tugs which is the emergency signal as he started his hand over hand on the air hose and life line to the surface and we also pulled on the line. He made it to the surface in record time and was OK. Had I made that dive it might not have gone as well because I didn't have the experience he possessed.

I had a very discouraging incident when attempting to leave the ship on liberty after ships knock off work one afternoon. Chiefs and officers were the only personnel allowed to wear civilian clothing off the ship, the rest of us had to be in a dress uniform and inspected by the OOD as we crossed the Quarter Deck. One day I had a couple very small pin holes in my undershirt caused by welding sparks and because of this I was required to change before leaving the ship. I was carpooling with a Ship Serviceman who worked in the laundry. On this particular day, he was driving and this incident delayed our departure back home to Portsmouth. When he heard why we were delayed, he said since nobody liked the guy anyway, he would get even with him. He steam pressed ground fiberglass particles into his underwear and to our delight; the Lieutenant spent a lot of time scratching his ass for the next few days.

In March of 1964 we were coming back from a port visit in San Juan when we were ordered to help the USS Antares AKS 3. After a three hour run at flank speed the Vulcan rendezvoused with the Antares and found her to have an uncontrolled class A fire in her number three hold. I joined the Vulcan's rescue and assistance team of fire fighters who were dispatched to relieve the ships personnel who were exhausted. The fire was so hot it had burned the paint off the side of the ship and the deck was hot enough to boil water. It was determined immediately why the fire burned out of control, the ships personnel could not get to the source of the fire. They were spraying water into the large open hatch from the main deck which was causing the ship to list. The large volume of water was doing nothing to extinguish the flames. There were bails of rags, cotton swabs and other combustibles which were producing thick toxic smoke requiring Oxygen Breathing

Apparatuses (OBA). The few onboard OBAs that were in working condition had all the canisters depleted and without them it was impossible to reach the source. We were equipped and made progress immediately by entering the hold and securing the first of several decks. We fought the fire and dewatered the space putting the ship back on even keel and ready to get underway on her own power. It had taken us from mid-afternoon on the twenty seventh to early hours of the twenty eighth to accomplish this and with no serious injuries to personnel. Everyone received glowing remarks in the commendations we were given upon arrival in Norfolk.

I figured it was time to go back to sea for a couple reasons; one being the crap hard working, devoted sailors had to take to get along with the assholes in charge. The other was because I felt I had accomplished all that was possible on the Vulcan and I needed to move on. However, I knew if I formally requested a transfer it would be disapproved. I went to the Type Commander's staff and inquired as to what SERVLANT ship was in need of a first class Ship Fitter who was also a diver. Before long I received orders to a sea going tug scheduled for a Caribbean cruise. I received orders to the USS Papago ATF 160 in June 1964 after serving sixteen months of a twenty four month tour on the good ship Vulcan.

USS Papago ATF 160

The Papago was commissioned October 1945 and Decommissioned July 1992. She carried a complement of sixty eight crew members, of which three were divers, two Chiefs and six officers. The Papago's primary mission was towing but she is also equipped for salvage work including re-floating grounded vessels. The Papago has towed large self-propelled cranes and ships, some as far as Europe. She assisted with the refloating of the USS Missouri grounded in the Chesapeake Bay in 1950.

I reported aboard in June 1964 and was assigned to the R division as the division officer, the Damage Control Assistant to the Chief Engineer and stood Junior Officer of the Deck watches underway and also engineering officer of the watch when needed. In port I stood duty engineering officer and master at arms.

We deployed to the Caribbean during the Dominican Republic crisis and received small arms fire while steaming close to land. We also pulled targets for other ships to practice gunnery exercises and although the ships were not supposed to hit the target, it sometimes happened. When it did, I would have to make repairs to the target so it could be placed back into service quickly. On at least one occasion a large round hit a couple hundred feet in front of us so the Captain radioed the ship to inform them and they responded "stand by, another round is on the way". As it turned out the other round hit close to the target which we normally towed a safe distance aft of us. We would also participate in off shore guard duty by going back and forth close to the Gitmo Naval Base channel. Of all the at sea exercises, this was the most relaxing but boring. It did afford those who wanted to fish the opportunity to troll because our speed over ground was the ideal trolling speed of two or three knots, just enough turns to maintain steerage.

Tragedy struck one evening while we were tied up at a pier to enable the crew to have a little time ashore. I had the duty that evening and was telling sea stories with the ships corpsman and was about to turn in when a ruckus on the quarter deck caught our attention. We both ran out the double hatch where we were met by the young man standing watch on the gangway. He informed us a man had just fallen into the water and immediately went under and had not surfaced. I notified the Command Duty Officer (CDO) who immediately called and alerted the base divers while another diver and I gathered our equipment. We were joined by the base divers and found the sailor floating face down at a forty five degree angle with only his toes touching the bottom. He apparently hit his head on a pier piling when he fell and went straight to the bottom. It was difficult searching for him due to the dark water and poor visibility. He had drifted several yards from where he entered the water so it took us a couple of hours to find him. As the duty MAA that evening I had to assist his Division Officer with the inventory of his locker and packing his personal possessions to send to his wife. What we found in his locker started a long discussion between the two of us about what to do with the letters and pictures from girlfriends. For the sake of his wife we decided it best not to include these in the package sent home.

Our Commanding officer was a LT (Line Officer), commissioned via NESUP, a program available to those enlisted personnel who qualified. The Navy pays for the selectee to attend college and be commissioned upon graduating.

We returned from the cruise in time for a promotion ceremony and initiation at the Chiefs Club for one of our sailors who was being advanced. When he was brought back to the ship, it was after working hours but those in the duty section decided to continue with the initiation by throwing the newly selected CPO over the side. It was a bad idea because he drowned. The Commanding Officer was interviewed and I think reprimanded for the two deaths. He retired sooner than he planned because his career was severely damaged by those two deaths. Our paths crossed again when we both were selling real estate. He was a good skipper and I really liked him both in and out of the Navy. In fact Captain Roberts was well liked by all hands because he ran a tight ship and everyone knew where they stood and what was expected of them. He proved to be a man of his word and when he gave an order he expected it to be carried out. A good example was when we were returning from a Caribbean cruise. He passed the word for all hands to hold field day in their spaces so he could grant liberty call as soon as the gang way was in place. Imagine how surprised and disappointed we all were when the word was passed for the "special sea and anchor detail" to man their stations. He had held an informal inspection and decided the ship had not been sufficiently cleaned so he was giving us more time to complete his field day order.

We were towing a ship out of the reserve fleet in Wilmington North Carolina when we had an accident which caused me and my helper several hours of hard work when we returned to Little Creek. We were advised to wait until a river pilot was available to guide us safely out of the port and down the river. The pilot was late getting aboard so Captain Roberts decided to get underway with the old Liberty Class ship in tow without the pilot. We were towing at close stay which was necessary due to the narrowness of the river and sharp bends that made navigation hazardous especially with a tow. At one of the bends, we had to back down to avoid going aground and when we did our tow collided to the port side of the stern damaging about eight feet of rub rail. The Captain informed me that I would be making the necessary repairs. He acquired the eight inch pipe for us and we commenced making the repairs which was no big deal. We spent the largest portion of two days finishing the repair. There was another occasion for me to make repairs. He had authorized the use of our motor whale boat for a fishing trip and it was damaged. We were able to make the repairs before anyone other than us knew about it.

We were tied up in San Juan P.R. when I was informed I had been selected for Chief. Since it was time for me to ship over again, I requested a school. This time it was to the Non Destructive Testing course, a Class C school at the Service School Command Annex in San Diego.

I received orders to the school in June 1965 with "for further transfer orders" to the USS Markab AR 23 home ported in Alameda, California.

The school was new and was established due to the sinking of a submarine, the USS Thresher SSN 593 in 1963. The sub was located and pictures taken a month after sinking and two special study groups were formed as a result. The first was a Court of Inquiry which attributed the probable cause to a piping system failure. The second was the Deep Submergence Review Group who initiated changes. One of these groups included teaching Non-destructive testing procedures to assure the quality of installations and repairs. The repairs to vital systems were to be tested on submarines and all other vessels as well. At that time it was their conclusion the sinking was caused by a silver brazed piping joint developing a leak which sprayed salt water onto electrical equipment resulting in the reactor shutting down. Years later a different theory was developed under the watchful eye of the father of the nuclear Navy, Admiral Rickover. Regardless of the exact cause NDT was necessary to prevent future system failures through quality assurance inspections.

The school trained us in the methods and equipment to test systems with magnetic partial (MT) ultra sound (UT) dye penetrate (PT) and x-ray (RT). X-ray was performed with both stationary, in shop machinery, and radioactive isotopes of Iridium 192 and Cobalt 60 for field work. We were taught to use a slide rule because it was necessary in order to figure the time, distance and shielding required in preventing over exposure. Figuring how to avoid contamination based on the source we were using at the time was critical. We all graduated with an Atomic Energy Commission license and certified in every procedure except film reading which wasn't offered.

We had several instructors both Chiefs and Officers and one who was a civilian college professor who taught part time. The training was advanced and it would be safe to say the most in depth of any school I had attended. The Atomic Energy Commission license was also the hardest test I had ever taken but we all passed because we were ready due to the quality of training we received.

USS Markab AR 23

She was commissioned in 1940 as the SS Mormac Penn in the Maritime Service as a C3 cargo ship. She was acquired by the Navy in June 1941, Commissioned as USS Markab AK 31, reclassified as the AD 21 in Jan 1942. After WWII she was placed in the service of Occupation and China service - FAR EAST. Markab was placed in and out of service twice, the last time she was placed into service was in July 1960 as the AR 23 and decommissioned in December 1969.

I reported aboard the AR 23 in Alameda, CA on a cold, foggy night in December 1965 and was greeted by a Senior Chief Ship Fitter who was standing the Quarter Deck watch as the OOD. To say he was glad to see me would be an understatement because while I was saluting and requesting permission to come on board, he gave me a big hug and declared me his relief as the pipe shop supervisor. I would later learn why he was so glad to see me joining the R1 Division as a Chief Ship Fitter with a pipe fitter background, HP welder and certified Nondestructive Testing school graduate. The messenger led me to the CPO quarters which were adjacent to the Mess and since nobody was awake, I found an empty bunk and crashed.

I woke fairly early but after reveille because the lights were on and I could see this very large dress blue jacket hanging on the edge of the rack above mine. I swear that was the largest coat I had ever seen and I couldn't resist putting it on just to see if it was as large as it looked and it was. There I was standing in my underwear with this large coat hanging down to my knees when this very loud voice from the top bunk yelled, what the hell you doing with my coat? When his feet hit the deck and he stood up I wondered how he ever got into that coat, the guy was huge. Very soon I heard his nickname among the other Chiefs was Tiny, to all others he was Chief Raeburn. He was six foot six inches tall, weighed 260 pounds and was the ship fitter in charge of the heavy plate and sheet metal shop. The next morning was Thursday and I went to the Mess for breakfast and met all of the Chiefs who were not on liberty. There I met a Chief Molder who I noticed was staring at me. From that time until I transferred he referred to me as the teen aged Chief. By this time I was 27 years old, had served on two aircraft carriers, a repair ship and a sea going tug. I guess I did look young for my age and I was much younger than any of the other Chiefs. Senior Chief Payne, who I met coming onboard took me to the pipe shop after breakfast to meet the troops and for them to meet their new boss. The shop was located at the bottom of a large shaft accessible by lower decks and also from the main deck to facilitate the mechanical transfer of materials. After muster (roll call) Payne and I went into the small office used for paper work requirements and went over all the details of the men assigned to the shop. That's when I was informed the reason Payne was so glad to see me and be relieved. Almost half of the shop personnel were either in the brig or restricted to the ship for disciplinary reasons. This situation plus the run down appearance of the shop was a good indication of what I was going to be faced with. I spent the next two months preparing for a long deployment to the Western Pacific. I already knew what was going to happen when we arrived at our first port and what we would need to successfully accomplish our mission.

The shop was well equipped and much larger than on the Independence. The Supply Department's pipe stowage rack was located in the shop and so were the pipe flanges, both with ample stowage space to meet the needs of the work ahead. Although the responsibility of maintaining an accurate inventory was passed on to me, it was well worth the extra work. The stowage arrangement facilitated the expedience of repairs and eliminated the requirement for written requests to supply for materials. We needed to save as much time as possible because of the volume of work we would be required to perform. There were problems other than with the shop personnel and cleaning and painting the shop. Determining the required quantities and quality of materials we would need was really an unknown. I did have knowledge of what materials each piping system required from hands on experience gained on the Independence. However there were no prior usage records, lessons learned or anything else which could be used so to determine material required was an educated guess. Convincing the Supply Department to order what I felt was necessary was a challenge but not unfamiliar, I had been through it before. With a sufficient amount of pipe and flanges onboard and having pipe bending capabilities for up to and including two inch iron alloy piping we would have about ninety percent of our work covered. Estimating the materials required for needed repairs to nonferrous piping and fittings, especially copper-nickel for salt water piping systems is just as critical because of the extensive use of salt water onboard Naval vessels. The required material for nondestructive testing was already onboard including isotopes of Iridium 192 and Cobalt 60.

We only had to use the stationary x-ray equipment on board twice and never the radioactive sources.

My past experience working with, training and supervising a thirty plus group of sailors provided me with exactly what I needed to do in this situation. My theory that you cannot make a sailor do anything, instead you must make him want to do it. It proved to be the basis for the success in training and supervising I enjoyed with this group of pipe fitters. By the time we set sail to Subic Bay Philippines, all my men were on board plus a few new ones and nobody was in trouble. I had a leading Petty Officer First Class who wasn't much help with anything. His wife problems seemed to consume all his thoughts plus he required a lot of special liberty. However I was very fortunate to get a young, hard charging Shipfitter First Class on board just before we departed. Petty Officer Holton was also a qualified welder. I still find it astonishing that we were able to fill the large pipe rack, flanges and fittings with everything on my wish list and more. The Supply Department out did themselves with this feat and I gave them praise and recognition for the good job.

The time for getting underway went quickly and as we passed under the Golden Gate bridge I was reminded of the many pictures I had seen of the sailors on ships tossing their hats in the air as they went under. I was looking forward to the adventures which I was to experience on my first cruise to the Western Pacific, it was an exciting time.

Our first port call was Hawaii and we had our first tragedy of the cruise. We were all required to fall into formation when entering Pearl Harbor and my Division and several others were in formation on the main deck near the bow. The Deck Department personnel were in the process of lowering a motor whale boat into the water from its cradle using a large handled crank to lower the boat by hand. A failure of the locking device caused the handle to be slung over the superstructure of the ship. The heave handle came down and hit one of the sailors standing in ranks killing him instantly. Not a good start to what should have been a great weekend liberty in an island paradise.

Several days later we arrived at our first port to start the work of repairing ships which were serving in the war effort. I walked out on the main deck that first morning to see several Destroyer type vessels nested on both sides. By noon we had a pile of piping which required repairing and our target slab which was a large deck raised about a foot was full of flanged pipe made up in templates for replacement. This scene continued for the remainder of our stay there and for most of the remainder of our deployment. We also had work orders from ships alongside for repairs of fixed piping which could not be brought to the shop.

My days were spent wearing coveralls and working alongside my troops providing instructions and teaching them the trade. My leading First Class did the welding and I helped out if after hours were required in order to finish what we had put on the target slab that day. The welding shop which normally handles all the welding was in another location unlike on the Vulcan. It soon became evident that us performing the welding was helping to expedite the heavy work load.

About half way through the deployment the ship got underway for some well-deserved R&R in Hong Kong. Another Chief and I had become friends and the two of us took some time off to see the sights and do some shopping. We were scheduled to stay for a week but a storm was moving in causing us to leave sooner but I enjoyed the three days I had ashore.

When the weather calmed we pulled into Yokosuka, Japan and continued to repair ships, mostly Destroyers but the work load was much less. At some point we also anchored out which provided space for accommodating more customer ships. We also spent a few weeks anchored in Manila Bay continuing to do what we did best but again our work load was much less giving the crew more time for liberty. The American Embassy was a short distance by cab from the liberty landing and the Embassy personnel seemed to enjoy our visits. Their food was excellent and we were free to use the recreational facilities including the movie theater. The bar and lounge was great and they served beer which we were familiar with and before long the word spread and it became the favorite destination for liberty.

Back to Subic Bay and the same old grind for a few more months until our tour of duty ended and we could set sail for the States. Tiny turned out to be a real easy going, kind and gentle guy who would give you the shirt off his back. I remember going on liberty in Subic Bay with him one time and while we were having a beer in one of the bars with a band, a young Seaman approached Tiny and commenced picking on him about his size. He dismissed the kid a couple times but he kept coming back and it became apparent he was showing off about what a bad ass he was for his buddies. Finally Tiny had enough so he stood up, grabbed the kid by his jumper with both hands. He lifted him off the floor and tossed him into the band instruments about six to eight feet away. Good thing the band was on a break and also a very good thing the kid wasn't seriously injured.

We started our return after what would have been an eight month deployment, but the ship suffered a bearing failure on the main propulsion shaft causing us to pull into Buckner Bay, Okinawa for repairs. Since the repairs required parts and expertise unavailable onboard, the shipyard personnel and parts were flown in from Japan to accomplish the work. The delay caused the deployment to be extended to ten months duration. There was a Marine base on the Island and we were welcome to enjoy the facilities. There was also very good liberty at villages numbered one, two and three as they were called. We carried more than one vehicle on board so the Captain came to the Chiefs Mess when we were all eating and threw a set of keys on the counter. He wanted us to have transportation but warned us not to let him see it in front of any bars.

I took this slack period to reminisce about the events and activities of these past several months and what we had accomplished as a team. We worked unbelievably hard to accomplish all the work requested from every ship we serviced. We had a relatively small crew of twenty five men who worked long hours to make it happen. They deserved the gratitude and respect they received for their performance and for staying out of trouble the entire cruise. All those who were eligible for promotion were promoted. We even had one man promoted twice, once to Third Class by normal promotion and again to Second Class Petty Officer by early promotion. This young man displayed the talent and ability of a seasoned Pipefitter although he had only been working in the trade two years. The on the job training and hard work performed day in and day out in the shop and on the ships made all these young men outstanding pipe fitters.

We were on normal working hours while our ship was being repaired. We took advantage of the time cleaning and painting the shop and doing preventative maintenance on our equipment. When we were finally underway to the States I had an interesting assignment which was not trade related. The executive officer was looking for someone to perform catch-up work on personnel records. The Chief in charge of the Personnel office who was my buddy recommended me. The XO asked me if I would do it and I agreed so he had a state room set up for my use. I interviewed and gave the training, re-enlistment briefing, and other requirements to all non-rated and first term sailors onboard. It was interesting talking to all these young sailors and it kept me busy during the 30 days it took to get back to Alameda.

Soon after mooring at our pier in Alameda, I received a written at-a-boy and formal recommendation to Warrant Officer from the XO.

Something happened after I received orders back to the East Coast for shore duty which meant more to me than the XO patting me on the back. It was a compliment from a peer, another Chief, one I held in high esteem. The guy who referred to me all the time as the teen age Chief and until now I didn't know if this was an insult or compliment. He met me on the Quarter Deck as I was leaving the ship and while shaking my hand told me he thought I was a professional. He informed me he was aware of what the pipe shop had accomplished during this past year and he was proud to have served with me.

It was December 15th, 1966 and I was on my way to Portsmouth, Virginia and another shore duty assignment and a very interesting one at that.

As soon as I arrived, we started looking for a house to purchase in Chesapeake near where the wife's family lived and also where the schools were better. We purchased a brick three bedroom, two bath house a few miles from Portsmouth convenient to my new duty station.

Our daughter Kris had to be hospitalized due to her asthma. Our oldest daughter Kim had to be rushed to the hospital after running through a sliding glass door. Glenda served as a Girl Scout troop leader to which the girls belonged.

It was January 13, 1967 when I reported to the personnel office at the US Naval Inactive Ships Maintenance Facilities Portsmouth Virginia to commence the checking in procedures. Later that day I met my Division officer, a Limited Duty Officer LT Junior Grade and the leading Senior Chief Petty Officer who had a desk next to his. The Senior Chief was a heavy set fellow several years my senior. I was assigned to the R Division where I would be in charge of the metal trades shops consisting of heavy plate, sheet metal, pipe fitting and welding shops all located in one huge compartment on the accommodation vessel. The shops had all the machinery activated and stocked with the material necessary to perform the required maintenance. Our primary work on the "moth balled" vessels was to maintain water tight integrity and dehydration for preservation of machinery and equipment.

I had lost my diving qualifications while in school and the following year I served onboard the Markab but maintained my diving code number. The Executive Officer informed me he needed a third diver and supervisor of the divers. He arranged for orders to send me to Harbor Clearance Unit Two at Little Creek for re-qualification to Diver Second Class.

I reported aboard the YFNB17 which housed the personnel and equipment necessary for the performance of training, salvage, diving and other operations as assigned. It was dark and the lights were out in the berthing compartment when I checked onboard. I took an unassigned middle bunk on a three high tier and sometime later another sailor moved into the upper bunk. I woke early the next morning and a porthole above the top bunk provided just enough light for me to see a leg lying on the deck as I swung out of my bunk. After I realized it wasn't a real leg, I picked it up to examine it closer when Carl Brashear, a Master Diver and Master Chief Boatswain Mate who was black, also hit the deck. He asked me what I thought of his leg and I said it looked OK but I thought they could at least have given him a black one. He laughed and shook my hand as he introduced himself. I had heard of him as everyone in the diving Navy had but I had never met him. He was there as part of the one year evaluation process required by the Bureau of Medicine to determine if he was physically able to continue performing his diving duties. Carl was an interesting guy who had survived in an atmosphere dominated by white sailors especially difficult in the deep sea diving community. He went through diving school in Bayonne, NJ and graduated as a salvage diver in 1948 during a time when blacks were restricted from the use of many facilities used by whites. I can imagine how difficult it must have been to find another student to practice buddy breathing which was required in scuba training. Carl lost his left leg below the knee on diving operations serving as the Master Diver on a salvage ship. It happened during the recovery of a nuclear weapon dropped from an aircraft in a midair collision off the coast of Spain. Although I never discussed the accident with him, I heard a towing cable under excessive strain had parted and caught his leg before he could get out of the way.

Although we were required to observe regular working hours, there were very few duties for us to perform other than the evaluation dives off the pier set up for training purposes. To pass the time we engaged in a sailor's favorite activity, telling sea stories. Four or five of us were sitting on a large hatch during one of those bull sessions when the mess deck senior cook, belly robber, as he was known, joined us. Carl was wearing a new pair of Navy issued shoes made of leather and canvas normally worn by the Sea Bees. The Cook commented on how much he liked the shoes so Carl took them off and handed them to him, got up and walked away in his socks. The Master Chief did something else a couple years later which didn't make sense. We were at the Chiefs Club having a beer at a table with several other divers, two of which were also Master

Divers. Without a word, Carl took off his leg and threw it to the corner of the room. After another beer or two he asked if someone would get his leg for him and one of the other divers said, you threw the damn thing, you go get it. When it was time to go, Carl hobbled over to the corner, strapped his leg back on and we all left the club. I think it was at that very moment he realized nobody thought of him as a cripple.

I watched the Master Diver during the next two weeks and it became apparent he would not allow a little obstacle like losing a leg end his career. I have heard references made about a one legged paper hanger, but I never thought I would see a one legged man jump rope but Carl sure could. He could also swim like a fish in a scuba rig, in fact there was nothing he couldn't do, but the final test would come when we went out to make deep dives in a Mark V "hard hat" outfit. When the time finally came, we were towed out to deep water and anchored. The waiting period was necessary because the diving class in session was also making qualification dives. It came as no surprise to me that he surfaced and climbed the ladder wearing the two hundred plus pound rig as well or better as anyone else. Needless to say, he was successful in retaining his Master Divers qualifications and was promptly assigned to another diving activity.

We became good friends in the days we shared on our temporary duty assignment on the YFMB 17 and our association as divers in the years afterwards. I didn't see or hear from Carl in the years just before I left the Navy. I was retired and living in Florida when my daughter Kelly met him. He was attending a function at the Motel where she worked and he saw her name tag and asked if she was my daughter. Kelly sent me his obituary when he passed away. My wife Lil and I went to the movie Men of Honor, which was about his life as a Navy diver. We didn't watch the entire movie because we walked out before it ended. It wasn't even close to being factual and that was a shame. His real life adventures, struggles and achievements would have made one hell of a story and the movie could have been better named, man of steel.

I was also successful in re-qualification to second class diver status and was assigned additional duties as one of three divers at the command. We had an equipped diving locker and diving boat which we frequently put to use plugging underwater suction and discharge fittings necessary to maintain water tight integrity. Each ship was sealed and equipped with a bilge alarm to signal water entering from an underwater fitting which required our attention.

When the USS Liberty was towed into a berth we were required to insure maximum water tight integrity but not to seal and dehumidify the interior because it was not going to be treated as a ship with possible re-commissioning status. The largest project and one in which I personally had an un-nerving experience was placing a large wooden patch over the main sea suction grading using "J" bolts. This was necessary to enable removing the valves and blanking off the piping that supplied the salt water systems throughout the ship. If and when the ship was removed from our facility it would ensure the ship would not be flooded by the large volume of water which could come from the main sea suction chest. At least that was my rationale for having us undertake a job of this magnitude. The carpenter shop made the patch complete with foam backing and drilled the holes in accordance with our measurements. We made the J bolts from threaded round stock and attached them along with weights which could be quickly removed once the patch was placed over the grading. We left one diver and a couple tenders topside and I along with another diver swam the patch down and under the ship. We both had under water lights strapped to our wrist to be used to align the J bolts with the openings. Very quickly we had all the J bolts started and enough of them tightened to hold the patch in place. After we surfaced and rested for a while I told the other diver I would go back and finish tightening the remaining bolts. As I tightened the last bolt and started going back around to check that all were secure, I started to feel my movement getting somewhat more difficult. It didn't take long for me to figure out what was happening. I was being pushed down in the soft muddy silt which is common at just about all the piers. We realized we were close to the bottom when we made the first dive but didn't think it would be a problem. My concern at this point was how much lower the ship was going to sink since I couldn't swim in the silt which had quickly thickened. The tide was at its lowest point and would be shifting soon so I just had to be patient. I was in a Jack Brown mask with surface supplied air so I wasn't concerned about the air supply. The crew on the surface was more worried than I because one of the divers came down to see what was going on. When he reached the mud line and couldn't go any further, he knew I was pinned. Their concern eased when they started feeling tugs from my life line shortly after the diver couldn't reach me. They figured out what had happened and like me, all they could do was wait. It seemed like hours before I could work my way from under the ship but it wasn't nearly as long as it seemed. We got together the next day and discussed how I was pinned for safety purposes on future dives under ships. The ship was tied up with slack in the lines to allow for the tidal changes. When the tide started out, the ship moved further away from the pier and into much higher ground providing less space than when closer to the pier. This was the only explanation we could come up with which made any sense because when we started the job, there was plenty of room.

Our shop work load had increased significantly so the Executive Officer made a deal with someone to send us 10 men fresh from boot camp. In return we would teach them a trade and make sailors out of them too. My leading Petty Officer was a First Class Ship Fitter and a very good leader, one who could be called a squared away Bluejacket. He worked wonders with what he accomplished working with this group except for one man. This young fellow was a hazard to himself and others, because he couldn't seem to work with tools without getting hurt. Finally Petty Officer Haskell gave him a bucket and assigned him to scrub paint work. Before long he stepped in the bucket, and, with his foot wedged tight he tripped and fell. The young fellow certainly couldn't be assigned to work with others for fear of hurting them.

I got along with everyone at the Command and even became friends with the XO. The Captain gave me a very complimentary letter of commendation when I transferred. I made Senior Chief (E 8) and I felt I had been land locked long enough, so it was time to move on.

I requested and received orders in November 1968 to a salvage ship. The USS Opportune ARS 41 home ported at Little Creek. However, since I was a Senior Chief and there were not any billets for a second class diver I was sent to Washington D.C. to cross train to diver First Class.

This was my graduating class

The difference between second and first class is the diving depths, qualifying on mixed gas breathing media and much more advanced training in salvage, medicine and physics. I had the opportunity to meet my soon to be

Executive Officer, Lt Kenyon, who was attending diving Officers training at the same time. We got along together from the day we met and I believe we were about the same age. I don't remember what the occasion was but he asked me to accompany him to a party. I was having a drink when this man approached me and started a conversation. We were all in civilian clothes so during our conversation he asked me what I did. I told him and included that I was a Senior Chief. I asked him what he did and he said he was an Admiral and then he said he thought we both had the best damn jobs in the Navy. I told him I thought he probably did but I was still working on finding mine. He was a likable, down to earth guy and I enjoyed a long conversation with him before the XO and I departed back to the school

School wasn't easy and diving in the dead of winter didn't help any. We made a couple of working dives; one was to remove the two screws off an old Diesel Submarine. I don't know where they got the thing but it was good training in scuba. Submarines are very difficult to tow and removing the screws probably made it a little easier. We also had to go down river and using Mark V deep sea diving gear, enter this small vessel which had been sunk for training. We patched the holes in the hull, pumped it out and raised it. Another interesting bit of training which was much easier was learning to use the diving bell. This is a large chamber designed to be lowered and attached to the hull over an escape hatch of a sunken submarine in order to rescue personnel. The ASR vessels carry the bell and maintain qualified personnel to use it.

I made a four hundred foot dive in the training tank on mixed gas before leaving school but other than that all the actual diving was the same as in second class school. What we were taught in the classroom was more extensive.

USS Opportune ARS 41

The Opportune was launched in March 1945 and decommissioned in February 1996. She served in Vietnam in 1966 earning one Vietnam Campaign Star. She had a compliment of eighty-eighty personnel of which, six are Chief Petty Officers, fourteen divers and seven commissioned officers. She is over two hundred feet in length, has a forty three foot beam, draws nearly fifteen feet of draft and weighs over two thousand gross tons.

She is known as a work horse of the salvage Navy having worked many salvage operations, earning commendations from many sources including Commander of Sixth Fleet and the Chief of Naval Operations. The Opportune, could handle any salvage assignment with a compliment of 14 divers, salvage equipment and a hyperbaric chamber for use in diving accidents.

I reported for duty in March 1969 after graduating from First Class Diving and Salvage School at the Washington Navy Yard. I ended up serving two tours on the Opportune with three six month Mediterranean deployments. I served under four different Captains and with three different Master Divers during my thirty eight months onboard. We had an unusually high turnover of personnel especially with officers. It was almost as if we were a training ship.

I was interviewed by LT Kenyon, the XO, who I had met in school so the meeting was to review my record and discuss duties. After the XO interview, I met with Captain Gagne the skipper, who was a limited duty officer (LDO) LCDR. My orders to the ship were as a Diver but in addition I was assigned the duties of Senior Enlisted Advisor which was later titled Command Master Chief. I was the Damage Control Assistant and also the Repair (R) Division Officer and Chief Master at Arms. I volunteered to stand underway Officer of the deck watches

Soon we were underway on a Mediterranean deployment but prior to departing I qualified to stand underway OOD watches.

The Captain on this cruise was a difficult man. Some might call him an unkind individual who ruled very similar to the Captain in the movie Mr. Roberts. I had a

First Class P.O. making Chief and the Captain called me to his cabin and instructed me to keep him in his dungarees and working because there was much work to be done.

I'll never forget escorting a young sailor to Captains Mast and having to pick the kid off the deck after he fainted. Gagne was upset because the sailor had gone to sleep on watch and allowed an area to flood. He was yelling and screaming while feeling around in the podium for his gun, telling the kid he was going to shoot him. Hell, he even had me scared that he was really going to shoot somebody. Another time we had a young Ensign who was the Supply Officer and he chewed him out unmercifully in front of me and some others because he had put the wrong kind of jelly on the menu. In the movie Mr. Roberts, the Captain had a palm tree growing on the wing of the bridge. Since he loved that tree, some members of the crew threw it over the side one night. On the Opportune, our "palm tree" was a crew member placing a marble in the metal vent above the Captain's bunk. When the ship rolled so did the marble and the Captain was unable to sleep. It was difficult to talk to this man and harder yet to get any results. I bugged him during the entire cruise to allow the crew to rest on Saturdays. The crew busted their humps all week and they deserved the weekend to relax. Standing the watches necessary when underway was hard enough on the weekends. He never gave in and the morale never improved.

We were in the Med as the vessel for towing, diving or salvage work if required and as it turned out we were needed. Although most of my diving was Stateside, this cruise was the busiest of all three Med cruises on this ship.

Our first stop was Rota, Spain where the Navy has a base and it is typical for ships to visit on entering the Med. Since there is a really nice CPO club on the base, several of us went to the club when they were having an initiation for new Chiefs. We always had a jeep on board when we were away from our homeport, so we called the ship to have the jeep come for us. Since there weren't enough seats for all of us, two had to ride on the lowered tail gate. When riding there, it was necessary to raise your feet to prevent them from dragging on the ground. John Garlick, the Master diver, was one of the two riding there and he failed to raise his feet. The six of us hit the deck at reveille the next morning and when John realized the soles of his shoes were almost gone, he yelled out "what the hell happened to my shoes". We all had a good laugh about his misfortune because it was some time before he could replace them.

Our first salvage job required open sea scuba to recover twenty four dummy torpedoes fired from one or more submarines. Sounds easy enough, visibility was fairly good off the coast of Italy. However, these things were fired and landed in a very large area in over one hundred feet of water and we could only locate them by using hand held sonar. By making one hundred eighty degree sweeps from side to side as we swam in pairs, we could hone in on one and have a direction to proceed in. We worked out of one of our thirty five foot work boats assisted by two divers from the Explosive Ordnance Disposal Detachment. We used twin ninety bottles which contained more available air than one dive required. Each diver must gage their own bottles to make sure there is enough air remaining to complete their dive. There were sixteen divers and two stacks of bottles, one with air and one empty. Apparently I was given a set that was empty. I violated the standing rule requiring a diver to gage his own bottles, I made it to one hundred ten feet with no air. To make that even worse, the strap on my mask had broken when I put it on so one of the divers threw me his mask. So here I am standing on the bottom with an ill-fitting mask which was flooded and not enough air to blow it clear. I wasn't sure but I thought I would have enough air to get to the surface due to the expansion of air with the decreasing pressure of the ascent. The first thing I thought about was what had happened to my swim partner from School and it helped me keep a cool head about the situation. I made it to the sun shine a little more than pissed at myself and I told the Master that was all the diving for me that day. It took several days and many dives but we recovered twenty-three of the twenty-four launched. In September 1969 we were anchored in the bay of Malta when we received a request to assist a Maltese ship, the SS Kristine Pace which was on fire and burning out of control. We weighed anchor and proceeded alongside to help with the firefighting effort. It was apparent the ship was in danger of capsizing because of the serious listing due to all the water poured onboard by two harbor tugs in an attempt to extinguish the fire. I took a few men with me and had a couple pumps transferred to the ship's main deck and started dewatering all the spaces. The fire was extinguished and after several hours of pumping, the ship was righted to an even keel. Several of us received personal letters of commendation from the Commander of the Sixth Fleet. The ship received a Meritorious Unit Commendation from the Chief of Naval Operations that included a mention of our next job salvaging a helicopter. Our ship also received a key to the city presented by city officials to the Captain in the presence of the XO and me at a party in the ship and crews honor.

We had another ship which required help fighting a fire although not as complicated and it was one of ours, the USS Francis Marion APA 249. I missed out on this one because I was ashore and I saw our crew was already on the way to the scene as I was returning.

We were tasked to accomplish another salvage job, this time a helicopter off the USS Sylvania (AFS-2) in the bay at Palma Majorca, Spain.

In the foreground is the starboard boxed ells anchor which is used when laying beach gear for re-floating vessels

The Sylvania carried two of these Boeing (UH-46D) Helicopters used for vertical replenishment of ships at sea. This accident occurred when her forward rotor caught one of the ships radio antennas and crashed into the sea. The ships other helicopter rescued the crew who had scrapes and bruises but were OK otherwise. Another diver and I suited up in scuba and swam a heavy nylon line to the wreck after it was located on the bottom in sixty-plus feet of water. We positioned ourselves, one on each side of the wreck and passed the line back and forth around the air craft then tied it off. The helicopter was lifted onboard and later placed onto a barge.

I had cut a gash in my left thumb from the wreckage but didn't realize it until I saw the blood floating by my mask.

I lost enough blood to start feeling weak when getting back onboard. I needed attention for my thumb and as luck would have it our diving medical Corpsman had taken a young sailor ashore for treatment for appendicitis. The Store Keeper, a First Class PO saw the wound and informed me he could take care of it. He took me into the small sick bay, opened the medical booze locker, gave be a shot of bourbon and commenced sewing up my thumb. It was obvious he had done this before because he did an outstanding job, and the thumb never gave me a problem, and left a very small scar.

Our last job for this deployment was to salvage a Destroyer's anchor and several fathoms of chain she lost attempting to anchor in a cove off the coast of Greece in over one hundred feet of water. The Boatswain Mate Chief attached the anchor hawk to the bull rope normally used for towing, placed it in the water, paid out a few hundred feet and started dragging perpendicular in the area where the chain should have been. The bull rope is a two inch diameter cable on a large reel with sixty thousand pounds of line pull when engaged. The anchor hawk is a large thick solid metal anchor which is shaped and looks very similar to an Old Fashion anchor with an anti-tumbling bar which keeps the flute down causing the anchor to plow the bottom. If it hooks into something with enough resistance it will cause the towing engine to engage. It will pay out a certain amount of wire before it starts taking the slack back in. The divers are then sent down to investigate what is hooked. The hawk works just like a grappling hook only hundreds of pounds stronger.

The work boat was put into the water with the necessary divers and scuba equipment. Petty Officer First Class Danny Bagby and I suited up for the dive which required swimming the length of wire rope down to the anchor hawk or far enough to determine what was hooked. Since we were diving well over one hundred feet of water the Master, Chief John Garlick instructed us not to exceed one hundred twenty feet which is the Navy's limit for open sea scuba. We reached that depth but couldn't see the hawk much less what had stopped us. I looked at Danny and made a signal to go deeper, he nodded his agreement and we descended further until we could see the bottom. Much to my surprise the hawk was almost completely buried in a large mound of mud but not the chain. I have made deeper dives than this however what we did was violate one of the basic rules in diving. You should never come up faster than your air bubbles and we did. Later I learned how stupid this was because at the time I thought if we limited our total time of the dive, John wouldn't know how deep we went. He knew anyway and besides he asked us when we got on board how deep we went. We didn't lie and he didn't say anything until later when I started having signs of the bends. I confirmed it by taking a hot shower which increases the pain. As soon as I told John he put me in the chamber and took it down to 60 feet where the pain in my left knee subsided. At that point John proceeded to give me hell over the chamber speaker, probably not as bad an ass chewing as I deserved but enough to get the message. Danny didn't have a problem which isn't unusual, depths and pressure on the body can have a different effect on individuals. I knew a Master Chief who was being tested by the Experimental Diving Unit in D.C. by taking him to increasing depths to test his unusual ability to resist the bends. Finally the diving medical doctors ordered the test stopped for fear he would get to his limit and be seriously injured. He was already way beyond the acceptable depth and times the table allowed.

We never found the anchor and chain and concluded the Destroyer gave us an incorrect fix on the location where they lost it or it landed in a tight ball and was impossible to hook.

We returned to Little Creek and were met on the pier by several dependents which included my wife and kids, the Captain's wife, as well as our Squadron Commodore. There was a lot of joking going around later that the Captain shook hands with his wife and hugged the Commodore which wasn't really true but it did fit his persona perfectly.

In December 1969 we had a new skipper come onboard relieving Commander Gagne. We soon realized

LCDR Don C. Craft had a completely different style of leadership. He was a very stern Captain but one who displayed much more trust in his crew and his own abilities which were demonstrated by his daring handling of the ship.

We found out very quickly that Captain Craft did not like anything to be painted or trimmed in black. I don't know why he did it but we had a Chief Boatswain Mate named Blazek who was determined to give him something of a personal nature that was black. He checked out a five ton stake truck from base transportation, went to the salvage yard and had them load a very large old fashioned type anchor. He then drove to Crafts home in Virginia Beach, tied a line to the anchor and the other end to a nearby tree and placed the black anchor in his front yard. I'm not sure if the Captain knew who did it but he left it there and even said he liked it because it gave a nautical touch to his yard. I drove by years later after he had sold the house and the anchor was still there. The chief pulled another good one only this time it was at my expense. He transferred to shore duty in Minnesota as a Navy recruiter although I could not visualize this guy recruiting anyone. He called me at two am and informed me he had recruited a young eighteen year old that day. The Chief went on to say they were in his office and he was helping her celebrate with a drink or two. He then asked if I wanted to talk to her and even though I said no, he put her on anyway. My wife asked who I was talking to and since it was getting a little embarrassing, I hung up.

Captain Craft gave me a qualification letter and insisted I continue standing underway OOD watches and added in port duties of Command Duty Officer (CDO) after I was notified that I had made Master Chief. He also assigned me the responsibility for training all new officers who reported for duty to stand underway OOD watches. I don't think it was because I was the best Officer of the Deck. I think he wanted to emphasize the ability and knowledge possessed by a senior enlisted sailor. This would encourage them to use senior enlisted men as a readily available resource of information. I know he respected my abilities because he recommended me by message and without my approval, to serve on the six-man CNO advisory board. The six men would be dispatched to commands around the globe. All activities would be visited the first year to collect information on several subjects. The next year was to be spent briefing the CNO on the information we learned and making recommendations on fixes. I went to the Pentagon to see the selecting officer to ask that I not be selected and he was kind enough to pull my records from the stack being considered.

I had problems with two officers who were in training and standing Junior Officer of the Watch. The first was a young Ensign fresh out of school. After about three months of training the Captain started to pressure me about when the Ensign was going to be ready to stand OOD watches. The young man was very intelligent but he just didn't give a damn about the Navy and seemed to have a real attitude problem toward his duties. He had the basics and demonstrated the ability to handle the duties so I finally told the captain he was ready. He gave him a letter of approval to start standing the watch. There are two chairs, one on each wing of the bridge for the Captain's use when underway. On the very first mid watch (2400 to 0400) the Captain couldn't sleep so he went up to the bridge to get some fresh air. There, in one of those chairs, was Ensign Fleming sound asleep. He sent the messenger of the watch to fetch me, and when I reached the bridge, he took me out to one of the wings, chewed me out and had me finish the Ensigns watch. The next day after the Captain had calmed down I explained what I thought the young man's problems were and why I was reluctant to qualify him. That seemed to get me off the hook and I think it reminded him that his pressuring me might have put the Ensign on the watch bill too soon.

The ships size and the men assigned who are necessary to achieve satisfactory results differ drastically. On an air craft carrier the mission is launching and recovering air craft. There will be nearly five thousand sailors when deployed in support of that mission. There is room for a few slackers, men who are not the best performers or those who might not know or do their jobs. But on a salvage ship as with other small specialized vessels every man has specific duties and responsibilities with no room for slackers. Captain Craft had a unique way of handling a sailor who wasn't performing up to the standards his job required. We had a new officer, a Warrant W1 Boatswain advanced from Chief Damage Controlman. He came aboard as the ships Boatswain in charge of the Deck department. He was responsible for accomplishing all the many evolutions of his Department which required hands on experience and knowledge he didn't have. After a few screw ups within a very short time which required the Chief Boatswain Mate to correct, it became apparent he didn't have a clue about the duties of a Deck Officer. He was the second officer I had a problem with him while he was under training as my Junior Officer of the Deck (JOOD). He persisted in arguing with me about everything imaginable even though he had never stood a bridge watch. I finally had enough so I sent him below to find the XO and inform him I needed a relief to finish his watch. The Captain called our Squadron Commander, who was next in our chain of command and notified him he was going to put the Warrant Officer on the pier with all his belongings. We were getting underway and we were not taking this man with us. Again, the Navy in its wisdom decided that because divers were in demand, the only way to retain this one was to give him a sea going billet which required a diving officer. This individual should have established his priorities better by deciding whether he wanted to be an Officer or a diver. You cannot learn to be a Boatswain overnight especially on a salvage ship. He should have known from the beginning he was setting himself up for failure and we heard later that he was reverted back to Chief. There was another time a man was put on the pier only this time it was a white hat and again the Captain waited until we were getting underway before calling the Squadron to come get him.

We were soon tasked to do a salvage job which was much more in keeping with our line of work.

There was a barge loaded with coal which had been on the bottom for several years in the channel between the Hampton Bay Bridge-Tunnel and the Norfolk Naval Operations Base. It was a most unusual constructed barge shaped like the hull of a submarine, open at the top and with heavy riveted plate on the sides. After a couple dives and much discussion, it was decided the only way to get rid of this monster was to use explosives. We had a YD which is a small crane attached to the deck of a barge used for light lifting that was ideal for use on this job. We were restricted on the amount of explosives we could use because of our proximity to the tunnel. We were using haversacks of TNT with primer cord detonated with mechanical caps from a rubber boat. We soon realized that the max permissible would not do the job so we decided to exceed the amount until we had the desired results. We were not being reckless in doing this because the charges had to be placed between the coal and the hull which absorbed much of the blast. We didn't think this was considered by whoever established the max amount but we assumed it wasn't a diver trained in the use of explosives. The barge wasn't as large as we first thought and though it took several days and several explosions, we were able to get it down to the mud line sooner than we thought. As a token gesture of our work, I had several plaques made and attached an old rusty rivet from the hull along with a brass name plate.

Before long we had a real Boatswain on board and after a few small jobs we were given a most unusual assignment. Wallops Island is a NASA launching site off the coast of Virginia and from there a satellite was launched to film an eclipse of the sun. It came down in over three hundred feet of water and we didn't have any means of locating and retrieving it. NASA arranged to have an unmanned submersible equipped with strobe lights, a camera and the ability to latch onto the satellite. The control booth was set up on the fantail where the operator did the maneuvering of the craft after we lowered it into the water with our aft boom. They would allow two or three of us at a time in the booth to watch it work the bottom and it was unbelievable the type and amount of junk discovered. The satellite was located and the claws which looked much like a land crab's latched onto it and started to the surface very slowly. When it was within about twenty feet from the surface the operator stopped it. The seas were choppy and it was feared it could come loose from the satellite if brought up all the way. Two divers went down and fastened a line to it which was attached to the boom to bring it onboard. Later we were informed the film was not harmed but would have been ruined had it remained in the water much longer.

A short time after finishing this job we were dispatched to the Caribbean for duties involving target towing, off shore patrolling, and diving and salvage as required. Before long we were requested to provide assistance to a Navy Tanker. It had several feet of wire rope wound around the shaft near the screw. The tanker was refueling another ship at sea when it had to make an emergency break away. We used gauntlet welder's leather gloves and a hydraulic wire cutter removing small pieces to begin with until we could loosen it enough to pull longer pieces out. The job shouldn't have taken more than a couple of hours to finish but additional time was needed because the area of the wire which had parted had to be handled very carefully to prevent being cut by the sharp strands. After the job was completed, we departed for the Naval Station at Roosevelt Roads, P.R. Some of the Chiefs decided to go to the CPO Club which cost me more money than I wanted to spend. There is a custom which is recognized and enforced Navy wide. Anyone who enters the club without removing their hat must buy a drink for all who are present. To compound my embarrassment and cause me more static from the other Chiefs, one of the men with me put the word out that I was a Master Chief selectee. Needless to say, I didn't enjoy the remainder of our visit very much and neither did the Chief Boatswain Mate. He was invited by the Chiefs on the English ship moored behind us to visit them in their CPO mess. After they showed him around the ship they went to the CPO mess for a rum toddy which is allowed in their Navy. Apparently "Boats" had more than one because he was asked to leave the ship. They had a mascot which was a spider monkey and he had crawled behind the Chiefs head. He must have thought it was a rat because he grabbed it by the tail and slung it across the room. I ended up having to dispatch a couple Chiefs to retrieve him. We were underway the next day headed back to Little Creek and looking forward to our next assignment.

After being in port at Little Creek for a few days, we were called on to go to Port Everglades to assist a Navy Unit stationed there. We spent a week in and out of port and when we were ready to leave an Admiral in uniform came aboard to ride back with us for his active duty training tour in Norfolk. The Captain passed the word for me to come to the bridge when were about an hour out of Little Creek. The Captain told me to assume the deck and the Con from the Officer presently on watch because he wanted me to take the ship into Little Creek. I thought this a bit strange because it was always the OOD who was on the regular watch who took the ship into port. The Captain would not qualify anyone to stand underway OOD watches who couldn't maneuver the ship well enough to bring her into port or get underway. I soon found out what was going on when I overheard him tell the Admiral "I trained this Master Chief, he's really an engineering type". Our berth assignment was the finger piers which required our gang way to be placed on the stern. This meant I would have to turn the ship around and back into the narrow berth between two piers. I did fine, didn't hit anything, in fact it was a smooth landing. The Admiral even complimented me but I'm sure it was for the Captain's benefit. Captain Craft pulled this on me a couple more times, once again coming into Little Creek. He had me assume the watch because that was the only way he could beat me off the ship. I had to relieve the watch coming into port again in the upcoming deployment.

We received word from COMSERVRON EIGHT that we were to be dispatched to the Mediterranean to take the six month deployment of another salvage ship, the USS Edenton ATS1, that couldn't make it due to mechanical problems. She was one of three new ships built to replace the aging ARS vessels. All three were built in England and the Edenton ended up as a Coast Guard vessel. We were given time to take care of our personal business like making out allotments to ensure our dependents could pay the bills. We were not too happy about this assignment but with the leadership provided by the Captain and XO the crew's morale was improving by the time we arrived in Rota, Spain.

We were tasked to stop in Miami and pick up three barges to tow to Greece. They were needed for water stowage at a new naval activity which was being established. After mooring forward of the first barge our towing gear was laid out and attached to it and the other two were attached for tandem towing. There was a discussion between the Boatswain and the Captain about flooding the lead barge's forward tank to make it heavier and perhaps ride better. Captain Craft didn't think it necessary and didn't want to take the time to flood it. I believe it was the second or third day at sea, when at day break, we discovered the lead barge was down by the bow, apparently flooded, caused by the pounding it had taken hitting the ground swells. The barge is divided and reinforced by three bulkheads so there was no danger of it sinking unless another bulkhead received substantial damage and flooded. Our speed over ground was slowed considerably from that point on and we all had to wonder if flooding the forward compartment before starting out would have prevented the damage, probably not.

With the exception of a new Master Diver on board, most of the crew was the same as last cruise. The mission is always the same because we are deployed for towing, salvage or diving as required. The crew's morale was the highest of any deployment I had been on before or after. As a result the ship was cleaner, the crew was more energetic and the cooperation of all hands helped make this one of the better cruises.

We finally arrived at our destination and released the barges and proceeded to Naples, Italy. Naples harbor is large and seems to have several US navy ships there at any given time. In order to make more room they have a special method referred to as a "Med moor" which entails use of anchors and mooring lines. I was not the officer of the deck going into Naples but the skipper passed the word for me to come to the bridge. He told me to assume the OOD watch and take the ship into Naples harbor and Med moor to the sea wall. I heard the Captain tell the Quarter master of the watch to hoist the flag display "enlisted maneuvering" on the main mast. We were assigned a berth located ninety degrees to and at the very end of a long sea wall where several ships, mostly Destroyers where moored. I don't mind admitting I was a little nervous because the space was limited and I had to turn the ship one-hundred-eighty degrees, drop an anchor, and back down while paying out chain. I had to get the ship close enough to heave a couple mooring lines to the bulkhead and stop until the lines were secured. After that slack must be removed from the lines to enable the gang way to reach the bulkhead. It was also necessary to remove the slack from the chain with the anchor windless. We were now ready to put the gang way in place, secure the special sea and anchor detail, and pass liberty call.

Naples is like a home port for ships serving time in the Med. I know on all my cruises we never missed a visit and some cruises more than once, sometimes for several days. I visited Naples in the fifties, sixties and now the seventies and I saw a few changes. There is a lot to see and do once a sailor gets past the bars and the small children trying to get into your P-coat pockets. My first four cruises were onboard aircraft carriers and of course we had to anchor out and take liberty launches to the fleet landing which was very close to where we are moored now. On those earlier cruises we discovered two places we enjoyed and we always paid each place a visit whenever we went ashore. On Via Roma Street was a restaurant that served great American style pizza. The pizza could be challenged only by the street vendors of New York. Another place we always paid a visit was a basement bar, which was no more than a hole in the wall, but you could buy American beer. There was also a juke box with nothing but Marty Robin's songs. These were the country music hits of the day and the thrill of finding a place like this so far from a country boy's home was unimaginable. Unfortunately on this trip to Naples we couldn't visit the bar, it was closed and the pizza place with the brick oven had been replaced by a much larger and more upscale restaurant.

Many things in cities all over the world experiences drastic changes over the years and Naples, Italy was no exception. I remember visiting a cameo factory located high on a hill overlooking the city which was no longer there. Some things never change but just get better such as a visit to Pompeii. A city of sin evidenced by the revelations of the activities inscribed on the columns of stone and over the doorways. The city and all inhabitants were destroyed by an eruption of Mt. Vesuvius which remains a prominent land mark nine miles from Naples. The Isle of Capri is a short hydroplane boat ride from the harbor where visitors find many sites and sounds to enjoy. On one of my visits to Capri while on the Independence, we had the distinction of having not one but two Navy Commanders who were asked to leave the club where they were partying. One was the Chief Engineer and I will not reveal the occupation of the other out of respect for his religion.

I think we spent about a week there and the crew was ready to leave after taking in the sights and exploring the many things available for tourists.

From there we headed for Greece to join the Greek Army for joint operations off the coast near the small Village of Piraeus. This sea port is the closest to Athens and is used when the capital city is the final destination. I didn't take the opportunity to visit the port city this time. I had been there before, and also had visited Athens on one of my carrier cruises. We anchored in an area a good distance from the sea lanes going into the port. I don't remember what we did with the Greeks but I do remember our Chief Quartermaster going ashore and coming back late one evening. He had received an invitation to dinner from a Greek soldier. Apparently while there he over indulged in a popular Greek liquor. We woke the next morning to the most awful smell imaginable. He had brought back with him a pan, similar to a cookie sheet, filled with tiny, well-seasoned deep fried whole fish. I understood this to be a Greek delicacy given him by his dinner host to share with his shipmates. He had placed this on our dining table so now we knew where the smell was coming from. One of the Chiefs went into the bunk room and beat him about the head and shoulders with a pillow while another took his gift top side and threw his delicacy overboard. It was several days before our stuffy quarters returned to normal. We gave our ships navigator a nickname after that, "Zeek the Greek" although some of the others called him by names which are unprintable. We had another incident having nothing to do with the Army. Our Chief Engineer, a Warrant Officer (W4) was a salty thirty year Navy veteran. He was also a survivor of the Bataan Death March of WWII when he was a Second Class Motor Mack. He was given a choice of Ensign or Warrant Officer after the war and he accepted Warrant. He heard of an ancient underwater city, and decided he would take one of the ships diving boats, a couple divers and try to locate the city and maybe find a few relics to take home. It was illegal to take anything from the waters or any historical site in and around Greece. Although they found the ruins and spent several interesting hours exploring them, the divers didn't take anything. We finished the job we were there for, weighed anchor and got underway for another small sea port in Italy.

I had the mid watch and it was about 0100 when we started through the Straights of Messina. We were headed for Civitavecchia a small village I had visited over a decade before. Had it been daytime, the snow covered Mount Etna would have been visible over the port bow from many miles out. However, it was a dark night with low visibility when I first spotted the red rim of the volcano erupt. Within a few moments she spewed what appeared to be large Fourth of July sparklers into the sky. Mt. Etna is one of the few active volcanoes that frequently erupts. It is an amazing sight to those fortunate enough to see the mountain. I have been through these very narrow straights several times during the many deployments on different ships. It is always exciting to navigate the less than two miles wide channel at the narrowest point. I have experienced some tense moments when the traffic has been heavy. The Captain is usually on the bridge and available if needed. The OOD has written standing orders to call the CO when passing another ship at a distance of less than two-thousand yards.

I have some fond memories of this small community located between Naples to the South and Rome to the North. We moored to a pier at the end of which was a bar/restaurant patronized by the locals. They were there playing cards most of the time. In short order one of our divers, Ernie Fairbanks, a First Class Boatswains Mate who frequented the bar taught them to play nickel-dime poker. I happened to be there a few days later when a couple women rushed through the doors. I am assuming it was their husbands they took by the ear and lead outside and down the road. That episode ended the poker games for Ernie and I'm not sure how he spent the remainder of our stay. Ernie had a brother stationed on the West Coast who was also a First Class PO. Ernie liked to say he was in charge of the East coast and his brother was in charge of the West coast. If his brother was anything like him, I doubt he was in charge of much. Ernie is a guy we called drifty, a sailor traveling around with less than a full sea bag. He seemed to always have to abort dives at thirty feet because he couldn't clear his ears. One of my two shops had a door leading onto the fantail. Ernie had one foot inside the shop when I saw his Chief knock him through that hatch. Being familiar with Ernie's mouthing off, I'm sure he said something that pissed off his Chief

The Captain and XO were going ashore and since they would be gone over night, he left specific orders. The Command Duty Officer would be the one to decide if getting underway was necessary due to weather or anything else. If the CDO decided to get underway, the senior officer onboard would relieve the CDO and take command of the ship only after it cleared the break water. I thought that was cool since I was the CDO that day. That is an example of the faith he had in his crew and I don't know that anyone in the crew ever let him down.

The weather stayed calm and nothing happened which would require getting underway. Ernie didn't get any more Italians in trouble, and the CO and XO returned in time to get the ship underway as scheduled.

Admiral Anderson who was in charge of ships in the Sixth Fleet at the time came aboard the Opportune two, maybe three times during this cruise. We had a fully dressed out statue of a diver in a Mark V deep sea diving outfit on the quarter deck where the Admiral would board. On one visit I attached a piece of fishing line from the wrist and over the shoulder and stationed a sailor out of sight behind the display we called Jake. As the Admiral was being piped aboard, the sailor would pull the line raising Jake's right arm in a snappy salute. As soon as he realized it was not a live person, he started laughing along with everyone else because he had returned a salute from a dummy. I carried a lighter for years with his Commander Sixth Fleet title and name engraved on it which he had given me on one of his visits. Each time he came onboard I was called to the Wardroom as the Senior Enlisted Advisor to join the

Officers in discussions with him. The questions he asked me were about the crew. Other questions discussed, which any officer present could have easily answered, he asked to hear my thoughts and opinions. It was the beginning of the Senior Enlisted Advisor title and was catching on with all Commands. Later I was employed as PW superintendent in Cuba. The PW Officer, a Captain called me to ask my opinion on how he came across after making a closed circuit TV appearance. I'm sure he asked me for the same reason the Admiral did. He knew I would tell him what I thought and not necessarily, what he wanted to hear.

There were other occasions when I was called to the Wardroom. When in a port which required a naval representative to board the ship prior to liberty call, I would join the officers and also be briefed. I was required to gather the crew on the forecastle and pass the information on to them. This was also the procedure I had to follow when critiquing emergency and/or damage control drills. The Captain would usually stand on one wing of the bridge and the XO on the other, overlooking the area where I held the meeting on the forecastle deck. At one such critique, two of the junior officers, who are required to attend, started to leave. They didn't think the ass chewing I sometimes had to render as an incentive to do better applied to them. One officer was going under the wing the XO was on which was to my left when I heard him tell the young man to get his butt back up there. Then

I heard the Captain give the other officer passing under his wing a similar order but the crew couldn't hear them because they were too far forward in front of me.

I believe it was in Valletta, Malta where we conducted public relations tasks by volunteering to remodel the school grounds by repairing and painting the equipment. We also agreed to make an attempt to blast and lower large boulders in one channel to a ferry landing so that both sides of the landing could be used. We didn't have the equipment to drill into the rocks in order to place the charges inside which was necessary to break them apart. However the time we spent setting charges was not wasted, it was a good refresher in using explosives under water for some of the newer divers.

After we were underway again, the Boatswain asked me to do a couple jobs for him. There were several small round stock brackets called "lady fingers" which holds the life line in the stanchions all around the ship. He had ordered the material to enclose an area on the main deck for use as a paint locker. The danger of a fire and even an explosion from the highly combustible paint products being below decks would be eliminated. I had a first class petty officer who was a welder and who had made chief on this cruise. I offered him the choice of the two jobs and I would take the other. He chose to replace the lady fingers so I took the paint locker job. We finished both jobs about the same time and prior to entering the next port.

There was a channel leading to a city that Navy ships never visited due to the limited size of the channel and shallow depth. The Captain thought we could make it up the channel so he requested and received approval from COMSIXTHFLT to go there. We made it but I don't remember much about the channel or the city. We were too busy cleaning sea shells and other debris picked up from the bottom and lodged in the salt water suction strainer baskets. The plugged up strainers supplied salt water cooling to the main propulsion equipment and fire main pumps on the ship. We were lucky not to have any damage, but we could have if we had not acted quickly to clean the strainers.

We were moored in Barcelona Spain on January first 1971 when my advancement took effect. I had taken the test in May 1970 but had to wait until the last increment to be advanced The Captain held the crew in formation at quarters on the Forecastle and presented me with the advancement certificate. It was time for me to ship over so I requested reenlistment leave. I went back to the States on the USS Denebola (AF-56) moored across the pier from us departing January 14. The Captain advised the CO that since my leave wouldn't start until arrival in Norfolk and I was a qualified OOD to put my butt to work. I stood bridge watch from January fifteenth until we pulled into pier four at the Naval Operating Base, Norfolk. Standing bridge watches on the AF which is a larger ship is a breeze compared to the ARS. They have a manned Combat Information Center (CIC) which tracts all contacts and provides the OOD with updates every three minutes of all pertinent information. I arrived home in time for the birth of our third daughter, Kelly.

While home on leave, my former XO from the Reserve Fleet, called and asked if I wanted to go with him to a poker game in a hunting lodge outside Suffolk. They played several times a month in the winter and the games were usually attended by local business men from the Suffolk area. He made it sound intriguing so I agreed and met with him for the trip. I followed him in my car since I could have never found the lodge on my own. I did some gambling and left much sooner than the Commander and didn't lose any money. I was surprised to learn the place was raided by the police the following weekend and everyone was arrested for illegal gambling. I'm glad I wasn't there for that event because I would have missed my return flight to the ship and would have been absent without leave.

I caught the flight out of Oceana Naval Air Station to Naples, Italy. I shared the flight with several wives who were going to meet their husbands, some who were aboard the Opportune. I checked back onboard on March sixth, rode the ship back to Little Creek, then transferred in late April 1971.

I reported for duty at Harbor Clearance Unit two, Little Creek in late April 1971 where I spent an interesting and fruitful thirteen months. I received three unique assignments that were based on my performance demonstrated by firefighting, ship handling, diving and salvage experience. One of the assignments was to supervise fourteen divers in the recovery of the remains of a satellite which was launched from Cape Canaveral. It exploded over one-hundred plus feet of water and covered a large area within three miles of the shore line.

I was flown down to the Cape to relieve the supervisor in a C-12 which happened to be the General's plane from Patrick Air Force Base. An officer, Ensign Bill Weeks was already there. I took another diver with me to add to the crew already there. I completed the last three months of the job and it was determined that we had recovered eighty-five percent of the wreckage. The young fellow with me was a Third Class Petty Officer and First Class Diver. I wouldn't allow him to sit next to me due to his crude speech and behavior. The destruction of the satellite had been necessary because it was not headed for the designated orbit. The Russians must have heard of the mission because their trawlers stayed about three miles from us the entire time. They apparently had photographic equipment with the ability to see exactly what we were doing. I believe this because I brought up one small piece of wreckage and the Air Force Captain who accompanied us each day, threw a blanket over it as soon as it hit the deck. That turned out to be the highest classified item onboard the craft.

Port Canaveral had a small tug we referred to lovingly as toot-toot. We used it as a diving platform and to ferry us back and forth to the diving site each day. It was January and the weather was not always cooperative. We had a number of days when it was too rough to dive. The rough seas were especially difficult after the toot-toot quit running and the Air Force had to rent us a boat. The boat they rented wasn't the best diving platform, but it was a lot more fun to drive and use. I suppose the thirty-six foot Chris Craft sport fisherman was all they could find. It came fully equipped for deep sea fishing with bait, rods, reels, outriggers and even a refrigerator full of beer. The Air Force saved money by renting it without a captain, since most of us were experienced boat handlers.

We were diving in excess of one hundred feet of water, so the Ensign and I went to the Air Station to inspect their hypobaric chamber. It was a nice one but too far away to help us in an emergency. We were making repetitive dives after taking the required surface intervals which would prevent residual nitrogen build up. We had seven two man teams which allowed us fourteen dives of more than thirty minutes each without decompression. They had a good fix on the location where the missile parts came down. We had exact tracks laid out and had a line which was anchored at each end. We would swim along it and then move it over about six feet until we covered the projected area. When the divers located a piece of wreckage they tied balloons with CO_2 cartridges attached to mark it for the boat to recover. We encountered a time consuming problem with the shifting sand, especially after a day or two of heavy seas. If a piece of wreckage was found and couldn't be recovered until the next diving day, it would be hidden under the shifting sand. Again, we went to the Air Force, this time to request they purchase ouster rakes and small shovels to use to uncover the pieces. This situation also required that we swim the entire area over again and we did find pieces we missed the first time for whatever reason.

The Air Force was very accommodating when it came to fulfilling our requests not only with items we requested to work with but of a personal nature as well. We found parts and pieces of the satellite every day, some days more than others. Due to security requirements we were taken to the hanger used for staging the parts for debriefing sessions each day. Some days we were detained for these sessions several hours. The amount of time we remained was determined by the number and importance of pieces located that day. Since we were being deprived of our beer drinking time, one of the divers requested a case of beer be provided. The next day and every day thereafter there was a can of beer for each diver iced down and waiting at the debriefings.

We rented seaside rooms in Cocoa Beach and on days when we finished early enough, we frequented the nearby local pub. We had three rental cars which were paid for with a Command credit card. Many times we would race to the pub and the guys in the last car to arrive had to pay for the first round. On one occasion my car was in the lead when the car behind us took a short cut through a ditch and across a large vacant lot on the corner to beat us. Another time, when I walked in the pub, I saw the divers who were there, had tied one end of a rope around a divers neck and the other end around a post. The diver was on all fours drinking beer from a bowl on the floor. If this sounds as if it was a bunch of kids acting irresponsibly, it was. This is but one way they acted irresponsible. One Sunday we went to the club at Patrick AFB because they had a large punch bowl of free Bloody Maries. Few others were able to enjoy the drinks because the divers finished it off in record time. Our visit to the NCO club that day was ended by one of the sailors who was dancing with a young lady. Suddenly he decided he didn't want to dance with her anymore. Instead of leading her off the floor, he yelled out that she had bad breath, turned and left her standing there. Most of the fourteen divers on this job acted like a bunch of animals but I have never been on a diving station with a more competent group of divers.

After we were satisfied we had recovered all of the satellite that we possibly could, we were released. We then turned in the rental cars, which were miraculously undamaged, and caught the plane back to Little Creek. Not long after returning to our Command a letter arrived from the Department of the Air Force awarding the Command an Outstanding Unit Citation. It read in part "for exceptional meritorious achievement under extremely hazardous conditions". Our divers were cited for the invaluable contribution in the establishment of innovative techniques of lasting value in future operations of this type.

My next assignment was to assist a Coast Guard ship, the USCGC Conifer WLB 301. We were tasked to recover a large buoy which was one of the channel markers entering the Norfolk Naval Operating Base. I took three divers and went onboard the ship with our scuba gear. When we arrived at the location where the buoy sank the ship anchored and lowered a motor whale boat into the water with my three divers on board. After they made a dive, located and marked the buoy, they surfaced to get what they needed to attach to it for the ship to bring it onboard. When I observed the Chief Boatswain Mate breaking out three strand nylon line, I questioned him about the weight of this buoy when it was full of water. He said it would be no problem but I had my doubts especially since the line was going to be fed over a rounded area of the deck instead of through a roller. I figured he had done this before and knew what he was doing. The divers attached the line to the buoy and the Chief on deck took a couple turns around the capstan and started bringing it up. It was a sight to behold when that line parted and sent small pieces into the air and the noise was equal to a five inch round being fired. The divers took a wire rope down and attached it to the buoy and the chief brought it to the water's edge, allowing the water to drain out before bringing it onboard with their boom.

Only the four of us and those observing the operation knew what "attempting" and "ultimate recovery" meant which was in the letter of appreciation given to us. The letter also recognized this deed was accomplished onboard their Coast Guard vessel on Navy day.

I was pleased to see Mr. Salvage CWO 4 Ryder when I checked into the command. I was assigned to team one which was his division and among our other duties, we had the chore of training all the salvage ships on the East Coast. His tour there was about over and he would be leaving soon but not before recommending I take his place as officer in charge of the Division and training.

My first ship to take through training was an ATF out of Newport, RI and it was an interesting week. Typically, the training starts with the ship breaking out all her pumps which is a pain in the butt. However, this is necessary because it exercises the equipment and provides training for the operators. After all the pumps were run we made up two Mike boats, positioned one on each side of a decommissioned ATA hulk which was a small coastal towing vessel we used for training. I would take a position on the bow and using hand held communication devices, guide the pusher boats out the channel and into open water. We had a designated area which was suitable for grounding the hulk for a training exercise the next day. The ship was preparing the necessary ground tackle for our re-floating exercise while we prepared the hulk. We were underway on the ship in training early the next morning. The captain would lay one leg of beach gear which consisted of a boxed ell anchor with a shot of chain (90 feet). Also required was enough wire rope to keep the ship in the deep water. The wire is attached to the warping capstan forward and another wire is connected to the hulk and attached to the H bitts on the fantail. There are variations, but for training purposes, the object is to successfully lay a leg of beach gear and to apply necessary pull to re-float the hulk. In a real re-floating the two inch bull rope which is normally used for towing would be floated back to the grounded ship and attached. Two legs of beach gear would be laid and the wire rope placed over the bow if the ship were an ARS such as the Opportune.

The next evolution conducted after the ship in training has re-stowed the beach gear equipment is firefighting, usually four days to a week later. We used the same hulk to build a class A fire from old mattresses, wood and anything else we could scrounge up. I would have the ship come along side and use its stationary monitor to cool the deck and bulkhead. I would then have a firefighting party board the hulk with hoses and other firefighting equipment to extinguish the fire and clean up the mess.

Seamanship training which is taught and observed during the refloating and firefighting evolutions, is included in the critiques I would give to the officers and crew at the end of each day.

There were always mistakes made, in every phase of the training that I pointed out and explained. It was obvious the crew needed a great deal of training and it was just as obvious the Captain required more experience at ship handling but unfortunately, he would never get it. I was on the bridge when we came back to port and the captain was conning the ship. He was making his approach to the pier on the opposite side of where our barge was tied up. The ship's speed was a little faster than necessary because the wind was calm and the current was slack. It would have been OK if the proper order had been given to the man operating the engine order telegraph. The telegraph is a device that passes the speed and direction of the ships screw from the conning officer's orders to the engine room. Unfortunately, the LT asked for all ahead full instead of all back full. The seaman on the engine order telegraph realized this was a screw up, so he delayed passing it to the engine room. However, too much time had been lost and the back down full order came about the time the bow hit and broke the first of seven wooden pier pilings. My CO called COMSERVRON 8, his boss and ours, to report the damage the ship had caused. Meanwhile I rounded up the crew of the other mike boat and went to retrieve the hulk. When we returned, we were informed the LT had been relieved of his command. I blame the people who put young officers in command of sea going vessels without verifying they have the necessary qualifications and skills.

On another training exercise, a Chief Boatswain Mate and I flew to Newport, Road Island to provide salvage training for a Fleet Tug, an ATF. We were also there to evaluate the test of a new type anchor. The anchor was dropped into a very muddy bottom, and it was shaped to go deep into the mud. There were explosive charges set on the anchor in such a manner that would cause the three flutes to open applying holding power. We did not think it was a good idea and apparently neither did anyone else because

I never heard of it again. Another fun salvage project we undertook at HCU2 was a training exercise gone wrong. SUBSALVEX 72 was the abbreviation of submarine salvage exercise 1972. Our Squadron commander had a submarine towed to a point off Cape Charles, Virginia and sunk by flooding all the ballast tanks. I'm not sure but I think it was the same submarine I helped blast the screws off when cross training from second to first class deep sea diver in D.C.

The USS Preserver with the LCU 1490 along side

I was assigned as the officer in charge of the LCU 1490 with a ten-man crew of divers. The 1490 is a large amphibious craft designed to land machinery on beachheads in support of troops who are landed by LCM craft (Mike boats). The same type LCM boats we used as pusher boats because they have twin screws and engines, a flat bottom hull, which draws very little draft, and are very powerful. The difference between the two craft, the LCU is several times larger and has three screws driven by three engines.

Our job was to supply air from the two large air compressors we had in the well deck to blow the water from the flooded ballast tanks, which was supposed to refloat the submarine. It would have been difficult to bring it up on an even keel but it would require no more time to raise than it did to sink. I have heard the expression, "if there is anything that can go wrong, it probably will" and this is almost a sure thing in the salvage Navy. I do not know where the crew that flooded and sank the sub came from but I would hope they were not divers. If they were, I hoped they were on one of the ARS vessels and had to participate in bringing it to the surface. What they had done was flood the ballast tanks and unintentionally, several other compartments with no way to blow the water out. We now had a real salvage operation requiring our squadron to assign a salvage officer to take charge and coordinate the salvage efforts of all three vessels. My divers had already connected air hoses to the locations that had air fittings. They emptied all the water from every ballast tank and that is when we discovered it did not lighten the sub enough to raise it. We brought the hoses back on board but did not have enough room to coil them properly, so we had what looked like a well deck full of black spaghetti. We could not operate like that, hell; we could not even walk around in the well deck. I received permission from the salvage officer to go to Cape Charles, stretch the hose out on the pier or sea wall and coil them one at a time. According to the charts, there was a sand bar between our location and the beach. There was just enough water above it for us to make it across. I was not too concerned about running the LCU aground because the boat is designed to be grounded. We made it to the sea wall and started to work on the hoses finishing just before dark. Since we were to stay overnight, I left the First Class Engineman on board and the rest of us went to check out the bar and restaurant across the street. It closed within an hour, about the time they rolled up the streets. On the way back to the boat, we passed a Navy jeep, which must have been the salvage officer's. One of the men suggested we hot wire the jeep and go for a ride since it was early. I went along with it as long as the wiring could be repaired and the young fellow said it could. It took him all of ten minutes to have it up and running. We went down the road a few miles and saw nothing but a couple of rabbits. I was concerned we would use too much gas if we went too far, so we went back to our boat and called it a night.

We got underway early the next morning, crossed over the sand bar without a problem and tied up to the Preserver again. We had one other occasion to get underway from the savage site, this time to go back to Little Creek for the weekend. There was a period of inactivity while we waited for the pontoons we needed to refloat the sub. Anyway, it was Friday and although it was late when we arrived, we still had a nice weekend because we did not get underway again until Monday morning. The LCU is not built for speed and it was difficult to choke more than five knots out of the diesel engines so it took several hours to get back to Cape Charles. The salvage officer who granted us permission to go back to the base was LCDR Gustafson.

He told me we were not needed while we were gone, but he worried that something might have happened to us. He spent most of his time on my boat and he and I got well acquainted over the next several weeks

The pontoons arrived and after the necessary rigging was completed, they were lowered into position and attached to the sub. The diving officer from the Preserver was a limited duty officer, a Lieutenant Junior Grade. He came over to the well deck of my boat to discuss something with Mr. Gustafson. I was standing next to him during this discussion, and the JG kept addressing me by my last name, so I started doing the same with him. Gustafson knew what was coming because I saw him slip the headphone off one ear so that he could hear us better. The Junior Grade LT reminded me he was to be addressed by Mr. or Lieutenant. I informed him those members with more or less rank than mine are required to address me by my title as well. If you will extend that courtesy to me I will reciprocate with Mister or LT, otherwise, to me, you are just another dumb ass sailor. The salvage master put his head phones back on, looked at me and gave me a big smile of approval, I don't think he like the JG either. Another man who paid us a visit from the USS Preserver was the Master Chief and Master Diver. He was the only other black diver I knew and he came over to request a drink of our bourbon. I said we did not have any bourbon and he said the Engineer had told him we did. I sent word for the First Class Engineman to report topside and he informed me he had a jug hidden in the coffee container.

One other time the JG came onboard my boat this time he needed my help. He said they had been diving all night and had burned out his divers. I do not remember exactly what they had been trying to do but it had something to do with attaching the pontoons together. I had four divers suit up and we went to the Preserver to take a look at what they had. I made the first dive accompanied by another diver using their Jack Brown diving masks. When I got back on deck I discovered I had lost my diving watch. It wasn't a big deal since it wasn't an expensive watch but I needed it on this job and until I could get another. The JG told me to stay there on the fantail and he took off up the ladder headed to his state room. When he came back he had a Seiko diving watch which he handed me. I thanked him for loaning it to me and he said no, I carry a couple of spares in my safe and I am giving this to you Master Chief. It took about four dives and within an hour, we had accomplished the job. Later that day the salvage master was back onboard my boat and I showed him the watch and explained how I came about it. He smiled and said he supposed there were no hard feelings between us two.

The salvage ships had completed their work positioning the pontoons so we commenced applying air to them to empty the water. In the next picture the aft two pontoons are out free of the sub and we are retrieving our air hoses. They will separate the rigging holding the two together and prepare them for the return trip to Little Creek. As soon as the crews in the two workboats alongside the sub were finished dewatering the passageways and other flooded spaces, we retrieved our air hoses and headed home.

The extra flooding, which necessitated using salvage pontoons, was a learning experience for most of us. I know I learned not to use the damn things unless it was the last resort. Besides being difficult to rig and position there is danger to personnel on the ship and to the divers in the water. This salvage operation proved once again there are two elements required for success in accomplishing the job, leadership and all hands working together as a team.

Dewatering and unrigging the pontoons

The next time I saw the salvage officer, Mr. Gustafson was at his house when he called me to list it for sale. I was out of the Navy and selling real estate and he was kind enough to think of me when he received orders out of State.

I would have liked to stay around a while longer but this was my last job at this command. I felt good about my experiences at HCU2 but I wish I had not agreed to go back to D.C. I allowed several divers to talk me into going for the Master Diver's evaluation. It would be best if I were a master diver because I was pay grade E9 and could be taking directions from an E7 on a diving station. I submitted my request and it was approved. I arrived and checked into the school and already I felt sorry I was there. I did not think I should be there for two reasons; one, because I had never served on an ASR. The background duties which carry a lot of weight is having served as a first class diver on a submarine rescue ship. The two ships are similar in size, but the ASR has more diving equipment with more sophistication and a completely different mission than the ARS. I had more hands on salvage experience, and probably more diving time, especially in deep water than most divers. However, the second reason I should not have been there, was because most of my experience diving was as second class. I only had about three years diving experience as first class.

Something happened, which I was unprepared for especially on a diving station down river from the school. We were using students going through first class school to make simulated surface decompression dives. I was running the station and had my tables with time, depth, etc. made up on easy to read and carry paper but not laminated as I should have. The wind picked up and sheets of rain started coming down which quickly made my papers unreadable. When it comes to weather, diving is like a football game, rain without thunder will not call it off, so this turned into a complete disaster. I really don't think that screw up on my part had anything to do with my chances to be selected to master. If the truth was known the old timers who were master divers doing the evaluations had already made their decision based on my two major deficiencies. In all honesty, selecting master divers is an awesome responsibility. Careful evaluations are required because of life threatening situations and decisions that are in the hands of those running diving stations.

I didn't feel bad about not being selected to Master but I did feel bad about giving in to those who thought I should go for the evaluation. Upon departing the school, the diving detailer assigned me to another diving billet.

I appreciated the irony of my orders from master evaluation though. I was ordered to the USS LY Spear AS 36, to relieve the master diver who was being transferred. It was several months before a "real live" master diver came on board

LY Spear AS36

The LY Spears was a submarine tender, a repair ship servicing the needs of fast attack nuclear submarines. She was commissioned in February 1970 and decommissioned in September 1996.

I reported onboard in July 1972 and was assigned the R5 Division Officer in charge of the diving and rigging lockers. Our routine diving consisted of attaching a goose neck to the overboard discharge and draining the reactor cooling water into a contaminated tank for disposal. The riggers who were mostly boatswain mates and a few divers had primary responsibility for removing and reinstalling machinery and equipment requiring repairs. We had three significant jobs to perform during my six months onboard. The first was a water borne screw change out, next was removing five inch, three lay nylon mooring line from a submarines shaft and the other was making voyage repairs to a large gash in the side of a submarine's hull.

The mooring line was streamed behind the sub when she got underway from the destroyer and submarine piers in Norfolk. The first class boatswain mate was on emergency leave so his sea detail station was assigned to an Ensign. The line locker is located in the superstructure of the sub. This is where the Ensign stowed the line. However, he failed to secure the hatch sufficiently, and the first time the sub left the surface, the line came out. The line immediately started winding around the shaft and noise alerted the Captain there was a problem. After investigating, the sub headed back and tied up at the pier adjacent to us. We were notified and I sent a couple scuba divers to check out the subs problem. I don't know how many feet of line was around the shaft because it had melted into a large solid mass that had damaged the upper half of the rope guard.

We tried several methods, using different tools before we discovered what worked best. We modified a fireman's axe by cutting off the pointed side. Using one diver to hold the axe against the melted nylon and another diver swinging a heavy sledgehammer, small pieces started chipping off. It took a few days but the shaft was finally clear of the mess and close examination revealed the shaft was not damaged. The next yard period they would be dry docking the sub and then the rope guards could be replaced.

The Spear had a diving officer, who I saw very few times which was good. He also served as the ships Boatswain and was a W2 Warrant Officer. I think he was advanced from Chief Quartermaster and he hung out most of the time in the ship's Deck Department Office. He was not even assigned to the Repair Department as he should have been which is why the Master Diver had the duties of the R5 Division. I got the impression from everyone, in both the ships company and the repair gang, that divers were not well liked. My attitude did not help the situation very much, because I didn't like anyone who wasn't a diver.

I disobeyed a direct order, something I had never done before. The Assistant Repair Officer was an LDO Lieutenant with an attitude problem. The disagreement I had with him was due to a job he wanted my divers to accomplish. A submarine wanted to air test the gasket on the inner watertight door of a torpedo tube. The diver would be about mid-way into the tube with the outer door open. I did not know anything about submarines but this surely was not the way to test a seal. My fear was, some jerk with a hangover might push, pull or otherwise activate the device that closes the outer door and separate the diver's upper half from his lower. The Lieutenant gave me absolutely no assurance this could not happen, just the direct order to get it done. My response was in a very respectful tone which ended our confrontation. I simply told him if that was the only solution to determine if there was a leak, I would check him out a set of scuba bottles and he could put his ass in the tube. I was not endangering one of my divers for such a stupid job. I noticed how red his face was as he walked away, he looked as though he was about to explode. I didn't hear any more about the test in the tube so I assume there was another means of testing for a leak. I did suffer retaliation over the incident but did not know about it until the day I departed the good ship Spear.

There were many things I didn't understand on this sub tender and even more things I didn't like. I think I figured out why the divers were treated like bastards at a family reunion. We were from the surface Navy and just could not be welcomed into their fraternity. I didn't know many submariners, even though I was on a ship with a bunch of them, but of the few I did know I have met just one I liked and that was long after I retired. As an example, I had built a frame with glass to display an old flag that had less than fifty stars for the American Legion Post. An active duty Master Chief submariner saw it and informed me in a most belligerent manner that I had the field turned in the wrong direction. I disagreed because I knew it was displayed correctly but he wanted to argue with me about it. I learned a long time ago not to argue with idiots, so I just shook my head and walked away.

I didn't understand why I was assigned to stand watches on the after gangway. Master chiefs, especially divers, did not normally stand watches in port on surface ships. This was especially true when the ship had E6 and E7 personnel assigned to the same watch unless there was only one gangway. I cannot be sure, but I think I was the only Master Chief required to stand that particular watch. I never complained about it because I knew it wouldn't do any good. Several times I was taken off the watch bill because of my diving duties. This caused discontent among others who had their watches switched. One of the times was when a Chesapeake police diver was sent to us for treatment from a diving accident. I asked another diver, who was onboard to join me at the chamber and prepare to receive the police officer. When he arrived I witnessed the most serious case of the bends I had ever seen. He was displaying serious symptoms of decompression sickness. His condition dictated immediate treatment on the deepest and longest recompression schedule. I used Navy treatment table four to one hundred, sixty-five feet of pressure with bottom time, and decompression time back to the surface, totaling over three days. I questioned the men who brought him to figure out how the hell this guy got into this condition. What they told me was a text book example of why people should be schooled in the art of working underwater. When they told me he had been diving in sixty to seventy feet of water, I knew exactly what had happened. He said the man had been diving on and off for several hours searching for a body. He would come up for a short break or a bite to eat and go back down. All this time he was building up residual nitrogen caused by not having sufficient surface intervals between dives.

I did call the diving medical doctor, and by the time we finished discussing the police officer's history, the doctor arrived so I informed him of the situation. He agreed that we had chosen the correct treatment, and once he determined the patient had stabilized, he went to bed. The Doctor said the man would probably need additional treatment before he was normal.

I was on a day watch on the after gangway when the CDO walked up about the same time a destroyer was coming into the harbor. The CDO, a Lieutenant made the comment, "wonder where she is going". I told him what pier and the berth number she was going to moor. He asked how I knew that and I said she is displaying that info with the signal flags flying from the mast. I was pleased that I could tell him something of a nautical nature that he didn't know. He asked how I had learned the displays. I said I had learned while attending officer of the deck and ship handling school and standing bridge watches. I told him I hadn't been out of school long enough to forget what I had learned and had been using.

It wasn't long before we were assigned another diving job that required I establish two teams and we work around the clock. A sub, home ported in Charleston pulled into port and moored across the pier from us. A tug's screw caused the gash in her hull, which extended below the water line. We were informed the tug turned too quickly after taking the sub out of the harbor. Our job was to make voyage repairs to enable her to return safely to her homeport and shipyard.

A patch over the damaged area would not work due to the curvature of the hull. We located a large steel cofferdam patch at the shipyard in Portsmouth, which was built for a similar job. We had the cofferdam towed around and it was huge, much larger than we needed. Since time was of the essence, we were not able to wait for a smaller one to be manufactured. I took the night shift, gave the day shift to one of my Chiefs, and assigned an equal number of divers for each of us. We used a crane to position the cofferdam and attached wire rope around the sub's hull. We used a "come-a-long" to snug the cofferdam against the hull. This turned out to be more difficult than we had thought. We finally had it positioned exactly where it was needed to make a water- tight patch. It was time to commence dewatering the damaged ballast tank and the cofferdam. It didn't take the welders long to patch the damaged area. It was on my shift, around midnight, when we were ready to test for leaks. There was a tagged out valve, which required the captain's permission to open or close, that was needed for completing the test. I went to the CDO, informed him we were ready to test but needed the captain's permission to continue. He flat out refused to wake the captain but would get his permission when the captain was up and about the next morning. There wasn't anything left for us to do so I left word for the day crew that I would be back in time to witness the test.

A Norfolk policeman pulled me over on the way home and when I asked him what I had done he said I had made a left turn without a turn signal. I know he thought since it was late and I was in uniform he would get a DUI on his shift. He could see I hadn't just left a bar and accepted my story about working late.

The next morning we were able to dewater the tank, put enough water in the patch to test for leaks in the underwater portion of the repair without removing the cofferdam in case there was a leak. The repair held so we commenced removing the cofferdam as soon as the crane arrived. After we finished, the wife of one of the First Class Petty Officers who had worked the night shift called me. She was complaining because her husband had to work such long hours. I surprised myself by the way I handled the call. I listened and allowed her to continue complaining until she was done and then I politely hung up. I had another complaint, this time from the CO of the Spear. He invited me to the ward room for coffee and my first thought was, wow we are going to get a personal well done for the diver's hard work. I found out differently soon after the coffee was served. Apparently, the Captain had heard of the delay caused by the refusal of the sub's CDO to wake the Subs CO. I was floored by the Captain's response when I asked him what he thought I should have done. He was serious when he said I should have called the duty officer at the subs Type Commander's office. His manner of reprisal was very different from that of the CO of a salvage ship. He gave me a dressing down, but if the Captain of a surface ship believed I had screwed up, I would get an old-fashioned ass chewing. There would no doubt be some screaming and cussing, and it would not take place over coffee in the wardroom. Oh well, I'm in another Navy, one I don't much like but this ship was picked for me, I would never have requested it.

The diving job which was ready to start when I arrived onboard to relieve the master diver was a screw replacement. There was a new and very large five bladed screw on a pallet located on the pier adjacent to the sub moored behind us. The removal of the old one and the installation of the new screw was ready to begin. I informed anyone who would listen that I had never been involved in a screw change on a fast attack sub or any other type submarine. The word I received in response was "not to worry, your crew has done this before, they know what to do". The person I was relieving was BMC Reed who I had served with on another ship. Having known the man, it is very possible the ship was eager to get rid him.

We started the job soon after Reed departed and this new experience provided a new twist or two. Getting the screw off was no problem and neither was putting the new one to the shaft. I had a talk with the man who was operating the crane and informed him that this was a first for me. Like the others, he told me not to be concerned; he had performed this task many times without incident. In fact, he told me he had worked with my chief on screw changes. Installing the screw onto the shaft went well with the guidance of a couple of divers giving signals from the water. I don't know the first thing about changing a screw but I did know what happened next was incorrect. The nut had been tightened enough to notice movement of the sub caused by pressure being applied by the crane. I asked the operator when he was going to place the tense-o-meter onto the wire and he replied they didn't use one. It was standard practice to raise the sub's stern out of the water a certain amount and the nut would have received sufficient torque. Everybody was correct about the divers knowing what to do because they worked well together and with limited supervision.

We finished and within a few days the sub got underway. The first time they had occasion to back down was while anchoring in Bermuda. That is when they discovered a serious problem. The sub would not go backwards because the screw would not turn. I was sent to Bermuda along with most of my divers and the screw pulling gear. The W2 diving officer came with us although he was no help. In fact, I had to get him off to the side and request he quit clowning around with the divers. It was the first diving job I had been on with him. The more I was around him the more I appreciated his absence when we were diving. The base personnel were alerted and been informed of our arrival time and equipment requirements. Everything was ready when we arrived and we were able to start work right away. I thought it was the retaining nut that caused the problem but I was wrong. It was the key that came loose. We had a new key machined and reinstalled. After testing had been completed, we boarded a plane with all our equipment back to Norfolk. I'm still not sure about the problem, but the men in my crew, who were experienced, said it was caused by a keeper not being properly machined. If it had been, it would have released the water pressure and allowed the keeper to be tightened against the key. I think we were very fortunate there wasn't any detectable damage caused by the failure. As far as I know the sub never experienced any further problems with the screw.

The master diver who came onboard for duty was also a Master Chief. I had served with him on my second Med deployment onboard Opportune. It was now time to remove myself from the submarine Navy and the sooner the better. All I had to do was locate a ship headed for a deployment. Since sailors don't like deployments those ships are always in need of personnel.

I had gone to the personnel office a few days before checking out to review my record. I saw my evaluations and discovered they were good. When I went to pick up my records, prior to departing the ship, I opened the sealed envelope and discovered my marks had been lowered significantly. I asked the Personnel Chief who had checked out my record but he wouldn't tell me. I went straight to the XO and asked if he had a reason to change my evaluation and he said no. I told him of my incident with the LT. and then I told him what I thought of his ship before I departed.

It was January 1973 when I received orders back to the Opportune and I checked in the same day. I found the condition of the ship to be much as I had left her in 1971 but with a different Captain and several new crew members. The captain was LCDR Camp who had come onboard from the Staff College in California in June 1972 relieving Captain Craft. The Executive Officer was also new, relieving LT Kenyon. I soon realized this officer was not as proficient as the former XO.

There were several differences between Camp and the two other Captains I had served under aboard the Opportune. The most obvious difference was the fact that he had never served as an enlisted sailor. It soon became apparent to me that he was an inexperienced ship handler. He had never served as a captain nor had he ever driven a ship. Some members of the crew who would be making this upcoming cruise I had known at previous duty stations; a Boatswain, CWO 4 Perry, the Chief Engineer, and Master Chief Oakley Southers, the master diver who I knew from diving school.

I had fewer duties than I had before, Southers was the Senior Enlisted advisor. An Ensign just out of school relieved me as the damage control assistant (DCA) before we departed for the Med. I was placed on the underway OOD watch bill but was not required to stand in-port Command Duty Officer.

I did not enjoy this cruise as much as previous ones, maybe because I had less to do. Other than one salvage job we didn't accomplish much. A few things happened which stand out in my mind. I remember having the OOD watch when we were coming into port to pick up a tow of a decommissioned ship. We had a very strong off setting wind across the pier where the tow was moored. We had to turn one-hundred-eighty degrees in order to moor in front of the tow to attach our towing bridle to the ship's bow. I had learned from ship handling school or had read somewhere about the "poor man's tug" maneuver which was ideal for this situation. There was plenty of room so I pointed the bow toward the pier into the wind and dropped the port anchor under foot, with very little chain, to hold the bow in place. By using the rudder and opposing directions with the screws port back and starboard forward swung the stern around close enough to get a mooring line over forward and aft. The captain was on the bridge while this was going on and he was watching without comments. Later when we reached the Mediterranean, we were pulling up to the pier in Cannes, France with a still wind. Captain Camp asked the Boatswain, who had the deck and the con, when he was going to drop the anchor. The Boatswain said, "why the hell do I want to that"? He never bad-mouthed the captain but I don't think he liked Camp and probably didn't respect him either. There was one other incident, while in the Med, which concerned me regarding this Captain's ability as a ship handler. I had the watch one dark night when we were heading into the straights of Massena. The standing night orders were unchanged from Captain Craft's tour and I predicted there would be traffic in the straights. I called the Captain to the bridge by sending the messenger to wake him. By the time he reached the bridge we had visual and radar contacts which one of my watch standers was plotting on the maneuvering board. I would go to one wing of the bridge to use the gyro repeater to visually mark and verify the contacts heading. Although we had everything under control, I suppose the captain thought that because I had called for him, I needed help. When the captain arrives on the bridge and gives a conning order, he has automatically assumed the con and the time logged by the Quartermaster of the watch. The OOD remains with the deck and has all the responsibilities other than maneuvering unless the captain also announces he has the deck. The other detail in this situation, a course change was not necessary. Had a course change been required to avoid a collision, the change should be enough to show the port or starboard running light alone. This would make it obvious to the oncoming ship what you were doing and on what side we would be passing. However, before I could inform him that there was not a problem he started changing course, first to starboard and then back to port while he was nervously pacing the deck. There were a total of four contacts which I'm sure was why the course changes back and forth. I was able to quietly convince him we had the contacts on radar and their courses plotted on the maneuvering board. The captain kept the con but did not give any more orders. The contacts were still far enough away to allow us time to get another fix to insure the course changes hadn't jeopardized our safe passage. When we were out of the traffic and everything had settled down, I saw the captain looking over the maneuvering board. He was reassured a course change was not necessary because the four ships passed exactly as plotted. I think the captain thought the contacts were closer than they were and didn't see all four ships until he changed course. At that time he could see the course change was avoiding one and endangering three of the ships. As the Captain started to leave the bridge I reminded him he needed to announce I had the con back so the Quartermaster of the watch could log it. It wasn't a good night for the Skipper.

Nothing else happened on the deployment to compare with this. I think he had started gaining confidence in his crew and allowing them to do their job.

Toward the end of our deployment, we were ordered to go to the assistance of the USS Kennedy CVA 67. She had lost an anchor in deep water off the coast of France close to Cannes. We were told the anchor she lost was her only usable one. This added to the urgency to recover both anchor and chain. They left one anchor in the shipyard and the other one, which was onboard, was unusable though I never heard why. It was a mystery why the ship dropped a sixty-thousand pound anchor in water too deep for anchoring. Each link of the chain weighed three hundred sixty-five pounds. I would think common sense would alert anyone that a chain that heavy could not be easily stopped past normal anchorage depth. If anchored in an acceptable depth, it would still be recoverable when all the chain was out. When we arrived, we attached the hawking anchor to the two-inch bull rope that is normally used for towing. We started dragging perpendicular to the direction the chain was laid. We knew it would take some time to locate the chain and anchor. I think it was the second day of dragging when we snagged onto the chain. The Almond-Johnson towing engine driving the reel holding the wire has sixty thousand pounds of in line pulling power. It would have been useless to attempt a dive to determine what we hoped was the chain we had hooked onto. We engaged the towing engine and brought it up as far as possible. We knew how deep the hawking anchor was by the amount of wire rope retrieved. It was beyond the limits of one-hundred-ten feet the diving regulations allowed. We were very fortunate to hook the chain fairly close to the end of the chain. It required fewer hand-over-hand attachments than if it had been hooked closer to the anchor. The Master Diver asked me if I would volunteer to make the dive with him. This was necessary to determine, by the markings, which direction we needed to go in. Once we determined the direction, we could start the hand-over-hand retrieval using the two nine fold purchases (block and tackle) over each bow roller. I agreed and we suited up in scuba and taking strong underwater lights, we commenced the descent. It was determined the depth was one - hundred - sixty - five feet. The dangers of diving in excess of the maximum depth allowed, especially in the open sea is nitrogen narcosis, "the raptures of the deep" as it is commonly called. The effect nitrogen, under pressure, has on the mind can cause a person to swim even deeper or just simply wonder off.

I witnessed a demonstration at the Experimental Diving Unit in D.C. The demonstration was performed in the training tank. A diver was given a hacksaw then taken down to a depth that would produce nitrogen narcosis. The diver was ordered to cut the piece of pipe on the workbench, and while we watched, he started to cut his air hose and lifeline. The demonstration was aborted immediately, but it was a vivid demonstration of the hazards of deep diving using air.

We made the dive and were fortunate that visibility was good. We were OK after a precautionary ten-foot stop. Oakey decided the direction we needed to go in to attach the first plate shackle. The first divers utilized the bull rope as a descending line. This was also used to attach the heavy wire and slide it down with them. For all future dives, a descending line was attached in the location of the next bite to lift. In addition, the next two or three dives required decompression stops which were closely monitored and supervised by the master diver. We worked around the clock for seven days and seven nights. We attached a wire rope to the last link that enabled the carrier to bring the chain back onboard. It was an awesome feeling to have the carrier come along side our ship, which she had to do to receive the wire. If anything had gone wrong, we could have been crushed. However, it went well and the carrier eased close to us without as much as a bump. Once she had the wire onboard and some chain in the chain locker, we backed down. Once we were clear of the carrier, we turned to be plumed over our anchor hawk. We began retrieving it prior to the carrier bringing all her chain on board. It would have been a disaster had our anchor hawk been entangled with the carrier's chain.

We stood clear until the Kennedy had her anchor housed. We restored all our rigging and departed. This job delayed our departure one week so we were anxious to set sail for Little Creek.

The crossing would normally take about fifteen days but we stopped to refuel in Bermuda and spent a day and night tied to a pier. We had picked up a Commander in Naples who needed a ride back to the States. Some of us Chiefs, along with the Commander, decided we would visit the Chiefs club that evening. The Commander was the Commodore of a small fleet of Navy Patrol Craft. He was a salty old guy who started out as enlisted, and ended with the honorary title of Commodore. Because he had a good personality and sense of humor, he was the entertainment for the evening. He walked ahead of us and his stride was similar to that of Popeye the Sailor man which alone was amusing to watch. About half way up the pier he stopped, turned and said "ah, it's good to get ashore, pee behind a palm tree and get down wind of a pretty woman". There was not a palm tree or a pretty woman in sight.

We soon arrived back at Little Creek and would be getting a new Commanding Officer. Camp had spent fifteen months of a normal twenty-four month tour of duty onboard Opportune.

In October 1973, LCDR Fred would be my fourth and last CO to serve under onboard the Opportune. As with the other three, Fred had a different personality and style of leadership.

It didn't matter to him that every year I was the DCA we received the award for the best ARS trained in damage control. It didn't matter that I had received a personal letter of commendation from Sixth Fleet, ADM Richardson. Nor did it matter I was instrumental in the Opportune receiving a Meritorious Unit Commendation from ADM Moorer, the Chief of Naval Operations (CNO). It also didn't matter that my fourteen divers and I earned an Air Force Outstanding Unit Award for exceptionally meritorious achievement for salvaging a crashed missile. It didn't matter that these and some fifteen commendations and letters of appreciation were in my service record. What mattered to Fred was what he had written in my routine evaluations, "Master Chief Strode's penmanship could be better". I don't think I need to elaborate on what I thought of Captain Fred.

My last diving and salvage job aboard the Opportune was for the Army Corps of Engineers. They attempted to hire a civilian salvage company to raise and remove a tugboat that sank off Coney Island several years ago. The tug presented a hazard to the large modern tankers which, if hit by one, could cause a very serious spill. The cost was prohibitive so they turned to the salvage Navy. Since USS Opportune was the best, we were sent to do the job. We were underway in the late fall of 1973 with a full complement of divers. When we arrived, we anchored off Breezy Point, a short distance from Coney Island. It was snowing when we made the first dive. This dive was to evaluate what we would need to salvage the civilian tug.

We decided that bow lifting would be the best and most expeditious method. The shifting tides and weather had deposited sand that had completely filled the interior of the tug. First thing we had to do was remove the sand. Our salvage pumps and eductors were used for this job. Soon we had removed enough sand to allow us to start rigging the bow lifting and other equipment that would be required. The weather was not cooperative most days, but we did have a few good ones. Besides being extremely cold and light snow, the seas were too rough to be safe for diving. However, it wasn't too cold to trip out of the three-point anchorage and go into port for liberty and we did a few times.

The most difficult task was to get a chain under the bow and stern. This was accomplished by using a suicide nozzle to wash out under the hull. We then passed a wire rope made up to a chain that led back to the ship. The chain was then pulled under the hull and the ends connected. The wire rope was reconnected to the joined ends of chain, and brought to the surface. The wire was led over the bow roller and attached to one of the nine fold purchases. The stern of the tug was rigged the same and attached to the other nine fold purchase. To use the floatation of our ship, the peak tank was flooded which is the forward most compartment on the ship. The tank will hold several thousand gallons of water that weighs several thousand pounds. Once a heavy strain is taken on both purchases, the peak tank is dewatered slowly, while monitoring the rigging.

The tug was well off the bottom by the time the tank was emptied. The two wire ropes attached to the chain were secured with carpenter stoppers in order to release the tug when ready. That also allowed the unrigging and stowing of all the ground tackle before getting underway.

We were underway early the next morning, heading to our designated area to release the tug. We cleared the harbor, were clear of the sea-lanes, and in deep water, when we lost the tug just short of the designated area. Apparently, one of the chain bridles had slipped enough to allow the tug to slide out of the other one. She went, down into water that was deep enough not to cause any ship a problem.

We set sail on a course that would take us back to Little Creek, hopefully for a few days of rest. Although I had only served one year of this tour of duty on the Opportune, I knew I had my five years at sea and would be getting orders to shore duty. I called the diving detailer in Washington to ask where he would be assigning me. He informed me it would be to the diving school in Washington as an instructor. I told him I planned to retire in less than two years and was not going to spend the time in Washington when there were several billets open locally. He would not budge from his decision. I told him he was giving me no choice except to resign from the diving Navy. I submitted my letter of resignation from diving, which was allowed, because it was voluntary hazardous duty. I also submitted a copy to the hull ratings detailer and I received orders for shore duty at a local command for my last tour of duty in the Navy. I had heard complaints by other divers concerning assignments by this detailer who was a Chief Yeoman. It wasn't long after I was forced to resign from the diving Navy that a diver was assigned to the position.

The Fleet Maintenance Activity Group (FMAG) organizations served several important objectives. They provided expert repair work to ships utilizing naval senior enlisted personnel at no cost to the ships or Type Commanders. They also provided senior enlisted personnel shore duty billets as well as continuing on the job training by association with others in their field. This activity also reduces the workload of the repair ships.

I checked into FMAG personnel office located at the Norfolk Naval Operations Base in February 1974, the same month I received orders. Soon after checking in, I was assigned duties as the R1 Division officer. Our operation was consolidated and moved to a recently established FMAG, located at the Destroyer and Submarine piers. A Master Chief Hull Technician already assigned as the R1 division officer became my assistant. I relieved him because I had more time in rate even though he had more time in the Navy. I had another Chief, an E7 who had almost thirty years in the Navy and I used him to check out incoming job orders and other administrative duties as required. I had my assistant take care of all required paper work and stay close to the office to conduct the necessary business of the division. I would take care of all personnel assignments, hold morning muster at quarters and any required training. I would also follow up on work in progress being performed by the one-hundred-fifty personnel assigned to the Division. With the exception of one Petty Officer Third Class, they were all Second Class Petty Officers and above. The one exception was a female Third Class and I assigned her to the welding shop to help string-welding leads when needed. Since Petty Officer Tobias was the most junior, she worked harder than any man at the command but she never complained.

There were only two officers, the Captain, who was a Commander, and the repair officer, a LCDR at the command. All division officers were Master Chiefs, the shop supervisors were Senior Chiefs and E7 Chiefs. I had four shops in one large building. This is where the Administration, Commanding Officer, Repair Officer and the Division Offices were located. All the machinery was in the building for the heavy plate shop and ready to set up and start using. It took about three months to get everything positioned to facilitate the work flow. This machinery had the capacity to shear, bend or form and punch holes in mild steel plate up to one-half inch thick. Transferring the heavy plate from one machine to another required using an overhead rail system. The sheet metal shop was functional but needed some rearranging to better facilitate the workflow for maximum productivity. There was a First Class in the sheet metal shop named Fisher who had worked for me at the Reserve Fleet in Portsmouth. Fisher and I had taken a trip together back then to the Grand Ole Opera. We went there in his new Chevy convertible and I bought the gas. On that trip we swung by to visit my Dad and paid a visit to Dad's favorite bootlegger. This would be the last time I saw Dad, he died a short time later.

Fisher was now heading up the job of rearranging the machinery, which required relocating the sheet metal stowage rack. He and another sailor were leaning the sheets against the bulkhead when the metal sheets fell catching Petty Officer Fisher in the back. I returned to the shop after checking out a job in progress on a ship and was informed of the accident. I immediately left for the Portsmouth Naval Hospital where they had taken him. The doctor there informed me he had a serious back injury requiring surgery. I visited him again while in Portsmouth before he was moved to a VA hospital closer to his home in North Carolina. I never heard from him again after the move.

The pipe shop and welding shop were functional and didn't require any changes. The large, well-equipped carpenter and boat repair shop was located a couple hundred yards from the main building. It was functioning and did not require any improvements or changes either. In fact, it was already in full swing, turning out an unbelievable amount of production in boat repairs for the ships.

Once we had the machinery in the heavy plate shop set up, it also started putting out a lot of production. We took on some large jobs along with the small routine work. All the larger jobs required Planers - Estimators to determine material and man hour requirements. The job orders for smaller jobs, especially when we had the required material on hand, would be accomplished quickly. For the larger jobs, the P&E section received the work order, investigated and forwarded it to the appropriate shop. One such job was to install a large piece of machinery in the engine room of a ship. The heavy plate shop was provided plans by P&E for the foundation. It was manufactured in the shop and taken to the ship where a large hole was cut into the hull. After the old machine and foundation had been removed, the new foundation was welded to the deck. The machine, a large air compressor was taken from the Supply Department to the ship but it did not fit the foundation. The plans for the foundation were incorrect and everything had to be redone. This isn't the best example of the work we accomplished, but one that I remember well.

The welding and pipe shops were productive from the day I arrived and stayed busy most of the time. We worked on main propulsion equipment through the weekend if the ship was required to get underway on Monday.

Like other Supply Departments, drawing material was next to impossible because either it wasn't available or it took too long to procure. Most of the work performed on the piping systems was on short notice, and critical to the ships operational condition and readiness. We had open purchase authority and used it often due to the short lead times. This was due to the customers submitting job orders for repairs at the last minute or breakdowns, just prior to getting underway. It became a Monday morning routine for the Captain to come by my office after quarters. I would accompany him to see the supply Admiral at NOB. The Admiral would demand an explanation as to why we didn't go through his people to request the material used over the weekend. I would explain the nature of the repair and the urgency required by the ship. The Captain would explain the importance of the work requiring the open purchase of material. He would also tell him we didn't have the lead time to order through supply channels. He would usually end our visit by chewing out the Captain, dismissing us with a warning not to do it again. It was his responsibility to restrict open purchase, but he knew we would do it again. I had a Chief assigned to the supply duties and he had established a good relationship with the venders. He could have just about anything delivered any day of the week with a phone call.

There were usually one or more jobs being worked during the weekend and I worked many Saturdays checking the work in progress. The work was prioritized according to the importance of it being accomplished on time. I was fortunate to have very competent shop supervisors that I could depend on. There is no way one person could keep up with the work load being accomplished by one hundred-fifty troops.

Tobias the Third Class came by the office one day and asked if she could talk to me. She had heard that I had been a diver. She was interested in becoming a deep-sea diver and asked what she would have to do to become one. I informed her diving was not restricted to men, but she would no doubt be the only woman on station. I reminded her of the difficulty she could encounter working in that environment. She told me she ran several miles each morning, was in perfect physical condition, had good vision and was not color blind. A Chief stationed at the second-class diving school at Little Creek had worked for me on the Independence and again on the Markab prior to becoming a diver. I called and ask if I could bring her over for the required testing. He checked it out with his boss, and told me to bring her when the request for school was approved. She was scheduled for an indoctrination hardhat dive and a chamber run for oxygen tolerance testing at sixty feet and she passed both. She had already passed the physical examination so she was ready to start the next scheduled class. She came by to let us know after she graduated and had orders to shore duty as a second-class diver. I never had a doubt about her making it through school; she was a very determined young woman. I'm not sure if she was the first female diver in the Navy but if not, she wasn't far from first.

My oldest daughter Kim at age thirteen made a demonstration dive in a training tank we had set up in Portsmouth for a recruiting drive. The tank was used in diver training and was ideal because it had windows all around for good viewing. The difficulty in the dive was navigating the ladder getting in and out of the water.

I got along well with Commander Kelleher who was our Captain. He asked me for a favor one day. He had a commode stopped up at home and wanted to know if I would help him with it. I told him to stop by and pick up a wax seal on the way home and I would come by and get it unstopped. We took it out to the back yard, without making too big of a mess, turned it over, and flushed it out with a hose. Among the crap that came out, was a lead pencil wrapped in toilet paper causing the blockage. He looked at me and said, "Master Chief, the next time an officer acts as though his crap doesn't stink, you can tell him you know better". I held this Captain in high esteem because he was among the few officers I had worked for who had the natural ability to lead that made everyone want to follow.

During my last nine months at the command prior to retirement, the Captain would call me to his office every Friday. This visit was to encourage me to sign the papers he had prepared. If I had signed those papers, I would have advanced to Warrant Officer (W3). This was possible because the Navy had discontinued the Warrant Officer program back in the sixties to allow the Senior and Master Chiefs to assume those duties. Apparently the Senior and Master chiefs had not assumed, or been given the additional responsibility as anticipated. Attrition had depleted the warrant officers ranks and rapid rebuilding would be best accomplished by using qualified senior enlisted personnel. Out of respect for the CO, I called the Warrant Officer detailer in D.C. to ask about duty assignment possibilities if I chose to accept the invitation. The detailer said he couldn't say for sure, but there was about a ninety-nine percent chance I would be assigned to an aircraft carrier. I had a long and sincere talk with CDR Kelleher informing him of my phone call. I told him what my Navy career plans had been from the early days. I think he decided I knew what I wanted and his Friday reenlistment attempts eased off a bit.

I had requested June twentieth, 1975 for my retirement date because I wanted my pay to be based on longevity for over twenty years' service. This was especially important because my "Kiddy Cruise" from my first enlistment at age seventeen gave me retirement for an extra year that was equal to two and one half percent more of my base pay.

I rented a three bay butler building, purchased some welding equipment, and started a welding business soon after receiving orders to FMAG. The business grew and I soon needed help so I made the senior chief in charge of my welding shop at the base a partner. Although the business was a financial success, it was hard, dirty work. I knew that Ensign Bill Weeks at HCU-2 had a real estate license and worked part time. He encouraged me to get a license, telling me the work was good and the income unlimited. I was successful getting a license and started selling real estate part time a few months before retirement. It was June 20 and the captain asked if I wanted to have the troops fall into formation for a personnel inspection and retirement ceremony. I declined, opting for a simple ceremony in his office with my wife and three daughters in attendance. The entire event lasted a good thirty minutes and I was out the door, into my new Cadillac and back to work. My assistant divisional officer retired a few months later. I saw him once after I retired, and was surprised to see him back in uniform. He informed me he had difficulty finding suitable employment. I knew another Master Chief Boiler Tender in Cuba who had also returned to active duty for the same reason.

Captain Kelleher and I stayed in touch after I retired. He called one day to invite me to meet him at the Breezy Point Officer's club for lunch. We discussed several things of mutual interest, and then he informed me he had received orders to CINCLNTFLT to serve on Admiral Kidd's staff. He was to be in an advisory position to the Admiral concerning engineering for all ships serving in the Atlantic Fleet. It was a great job with advancement opportunities to Captain and beyond. He was very excited about getting the job. The Admiral had hand picked him because of the efficiency of the FMAG command when he was the CO.

He was on leave before reporting to his new assignment, but was called in to fly out to a destroyer to evaluate their engineering problems. He boarded a helicopter and was flown to the ship. Something went terribly wrong when they were lowering him to the fantail of the ship. He was dropped onto the deck and died from the fall. The circumstances of the accident were never made known to the public. I attended his funeral at the Chapel at the Naval Amphibious Base at Little Creek and it was a sad day for all who knew and served with him.

12 Executive Park
Norfolk, Virginia 23502

461-8686

DEL STRODE, GRI
Broker
Member: Million Dollar Sales Club
Res: 857-7604
Mobile: 625-8268

Circle Realty and Consultants

I departed the Navy without fanfare and started selling real estate with a passion. The Ensign, Bill Weeks, had retired and was working at an office in Virginia Beach so I joined the same firm. I worked long hours at both listing and selling homes. I made the Million Dollar Sales club the first six months of working full time. It is an accomplishment which was difficult to achieve, because the average homes I sold were less than fifty thousand dollars. You had to sell a lot of properties to reach that level. Most of my workdays started at 7:30 - 8:00 AM visiting sale "by owner" listings in the paper. I normally worked until 9:00 PM showing properties or working the phone. I also made cold calls from the listings in the paper. I would either buy the home outright, or list it with a guarantee to purchase, at the end of the listing period. Most of the time I would attempt to list the home through the company. What I did depended on the type of mortgage, sales price and equity. I preferred to purchase the home for resale, because the market was good, and I made more money. I found a deal on a car phone not long after I purchased the new Cadillac and had it installed. It was a Motorola unit which fit in the trunk and was the size of a suitcase. If I received a call at the office on one of my listings, it would be forwarded to me in my car; otherwise, the duty agent would get the call. The phone paid for itself the first month after installation. I wore the Sedan Deville out in three years, bought a 1978 Coupe Deville off the show room floor to replace it, and of course, had the car phone installed. It was a neat baby blue Coupe Deville on sale for nine-thousand-nine-hundred-ninety- nine dollars. By this time, I had taken the test and passed the Brokers examination. A broker's license was necessary to start my own business which I did a while later. I continued working long hours and quickly made a profitable business out of the small company. I had several rentals that were a management headache. I also started the first "help you sell" business in the Tidewater area. I bought for resale several houses and made money on them all. I purchased one property near the Amphibious Base that I had to keep. The property required more work than expected so the required sales price was too high. After two years, I sold it to the Chief who was renting it. The eight percent appreciation per year was enough to show a profit.

I had heard the term "burned out", associated with many jobs, but this was my first job that the term fit. I walked away from a lucrative business and applied for a position at the Norfolk Naval Shipyard in Portsmouth. It was some time before the selection was made, so I started working, as the hands on supervisor, of the silver brazing section of the Air-O-Plane Cooperation in Norfolk. The company made portable air conditioners for use on airplanes before they started their engines. It was definitely a blue-collar job. I knew my baby blue Cadillac would be out of place parked in front of the building, especially one equipped with a car phone. I usually parked a block or two around the corner from the entrance so there would be no need to explain why I was working there. I can honestly say I enjoyed working with my hands in an occupation I had been certified in many years before. The two months I worked there were most enjoyable because of the eight hour work days. One of the mechanics working there was stationed on the Vulcan when I was but I didn't know anyone else.

I resigned from the Air-O-Plane Corp., when I was notified by the NNSY personnel office, that I would be interviewed for the position for which I had applied

USS Pegasus PHM 1

The NNSY personnel office set an appointment for the interview. The interview was conducted by a GS13, who was the supervisor over the scheduling and progress department, and a GS12 who was the manager of the progress section. I was hired for the job, WD8 submarine scheduler, and was surprised that the supervisor of that section was not present at the interview. The ten or twelve men I joined had the primary duty of making bubble charts. These charts were to be used to guide a sub through its overhaul or repairs. Sounds easy but the job required a great deal of experience and knowledge of various systems and the time required for installation or repairs.

I ran into the assistant repair officer from the LY Spear who was retired and working in submarines. I had not spoken with him since the torpedo tube incident and I saw no reason to speak to him now. As it turned out, several employees of the shipyard shared my feelings about this man too.

At the end of my first three months, I was asked to clean out my desk, although I was not given a reason I learned I had been reassigned to the Progress Section, which is where I was hired to work. There was an opening in scheduling, which was not needed, however, a pending vacancy in the progress section that did. I was assigned a desk in a room with about twenty others. The head of the section, a GS12, was in the same room but behind a glass enclosure. The immediate supervisor was a WS13 who sat in front of the glass enclosure. He acted busy by constantly rearranging papers on his desk. I witnessed some of the others around me doing the same.

I was assigned several jobs to follow the workflow, through the various shops, and to keep them manned sufficiently in order to meet their scheduled completion date. To say it was a boring; do nothing job, regardless of the importance, would be an understatement. I had fun joking around with a retired Master Chief electrician working at the desk in front of mine. He swore I was a Navy investigator because he said no one was hired off the street for this job. It was true, all the employees in this section, as well as in scheduling, were hired from water front, workers who had proven qualifications and performance in their trade. I was told that I was hired because of my ship repair background, my supervisory positions, and my several and varied duty assignments. I told this to the ole boy, but he kept insisting I was NCIS. When I was assigned to my first project as the manager, he told me that was proof. After that job was completed, my next assignment was as the ship superintendent of the hydrofoil PHM1 The retired Master Chief didn't say too much now, he was more certain than ever I was a "plant". It was unusual for Progress Section personnel to be assigned as Ships Superintendents. Their normal functions were to assist the Officers who were assigned that duty.

The Pegasus had gone aground in the James River running at high speeds while coming off the foils in too shallow water. I believe the craft was going faster than the Captain could think. Five million dollars had been allocated to accomplish repairs to both forward and after foils. It was soon obvious the funding was not sufficient. I spent a large portion of that just getting her into dry-dock. The shipyard did not have the docking blocks required Since the Pegasus was new and the first of her class, and the prototype for five more that were being built, we had to purchase the blocks. We purchased them and many of the mechanical and other spare parts from the Boeing Company in California. It took more than one truckload to haul the cradle to Virginia from California to use in the dry dock.

To straighten the bent stainless steel portion of the forward pod required taking it to the shop but it had no other major damage. The actuators which raise and lower the after foil had to be replaced and so did the mounting pads on both sides of the hull. The precision of the actuators when moving was critical and required optically aligned when reinstalled. Stainless steel bolts and other materials requiring replacement on the pods had to be purchased from California and were costly and time consuming. If they had known the scope of the repairs on this strange little ship, they might have assigned a more experienced superintendent. I guess I was doing the job well enough because they could have relieved me; however, I saw the repairs through to completion and sea trials. I really enjoyed the challenge of the position and the experience it provided.

Commanders (O5) were assigned to aircraft carriers with several other officers to assist and lower ranking officers for smaller vessels. I would probably have stayed at NNSY had there been even the possibility of getting a promotion and reassigned. I was informed that hell would freeze over before a civilian would be hired to do that job.

During this time, Glenda and I were going through a legal separation and I decided it would be best to get out of town for a while. I started looking at overseas positions and located one that I thought would be a perfect fit for me.

I applied for, and was selected to the General Foreman (WS14) position as the head of the Services Branch in the Ship Repair Department, Guantanamo Bay, Cuba.

Dry Dock AFDL 1 US Naval Station Guantanamo Bay Cuba

The base was leased from Cuba in 1903 and has remained in service ever since. It was populated with seventy-five hundred personnel in December 1979 when I arrived. It covers forty-three square miles and has gained attention since adding a prison for terrorists in 2002. It had a diversified work force, made up of contract Jamaican workers, exile Cubans, Cuban commuters, military and D.O.D. civilians. I learned I had my share of the mix among the more than one hundred I would soon be supervising

When I arrived, the Ship Repair Department's Planner-Estimator Supervisor met me. He was a heavyset fellow named Beckwith who loved fishing. He escorted me to the personnel office where I received the check in sheet and directions to the places I needed to go. I started at SRD with my Supervisor, CDR Cooper, the department head and repair officer. He was an easygoing type and had a likable personality. After completing check in, I was assigned two adjoining rooms at the BOQ. One room faced the street side; the other adjoining room overlooked the bay. It is customary to provide senior officers and equivalent civilians the privilege of two rooms when space was available. In Gitmo all civilians have a military rank equivalency assigned based on their pay. The equivalency is used to determine several things such as housing, clubs and privileges to name a few. My civilian grade level was given as a Commander (05) equivalence

I went back to SRD to check out my shops and working areas. My office was at the end of the carpenter/boat repair shop. This was a large, well equipped, building with large capacity wood working machinery. I noticed an antique Chris Craft run-a-bout with a new mahogany enclosed forward deck. I was to be in charge of the riggers, painters, tank cleaners, carpenters and laborers. For office staff I chose a Third Class Wave as secretary, and a Jamaican named Blake. He was classified as a motor vehicle operator but I used him to run errands for everyone. The Chief Boatswain Mate, who was in charge and awaiting transfer, remained in the office as well. I received another Chief to replace him and I assigned him as assistant Branch Head. He became invaluable because he was a take-charge leader, eager to learn how to handle a civilian work force.

Before long, I was assigned the duties of the dock master, the weight test director, and responsibility for the use of a one hundred ton floating crane.

I received notice from the Repair Officer that the USS Pegasus would be arriving in a few days and what would be required to support her visit. It appeared I was never going to be rid of this vessel; however, it turned out to be a great visit. I met an interesting officer, an LDO LTJG, who took a Commission from Master Chief Engineman. He was currently assigned as the engineering officer for the new squadron. He had nothing good to say about the Pegasus, in fact he complained constantly about his job and the ship. I heard later, after the Pegasus had departed, he reverted to Master Chief. His frustration was understandable because a Boeing 737 jet engine powered the hydrofoils and an Engineman does not know much about them.

The first tug I docked, I noticed a useless waste of the sandblast material. They would scoop it up and dispose it, then re-order the same amount. I submitted a beneficial suggestion to get funding to purchase reclaim machinery. We were able to purchase the equipment with the thirty thousand forty-four dollar savings, and I was awarded just over eight hundred for my trouble.

The Repair Officer wanted to make me the diving supervisor until I told him Navy regulations would not permit that. I accepted the collateral duties the Commander had assigned until he informed me I was to relieve the Chief in charge of the Structural Branch. I said I could handle both branches but I would require more pay to take over four more shops. He agreed and sent the new job description to personnel for reclassification. The classification specialist made it a WS16 position but the personnel director wouldn't allow the WS16 rating. Although I supervised several different trades, none were in the electronics field. I did get the WS15 grade and started checking out my new troops and their shops.

I found illegal activities taking place in both Branches that I was now responsible for supervising. Things such as the new boat decking behind the carpenter shop. Government employees using shop supplies were accomplishing this work. The paint shop was accustomed to giving away very expensive bottom antifouling paint to anyone who asked for it for private boats. The one hundred ton floating crane was being used to make lifts to private craft and placing them on the sea wall. The welding shop had an employee welding on piping obtained from the pipe shop. He was making handrails for a civilian contractor who was building a large boat from a kit. I suspected the welding had been done during working hours in the past, I know the material used was government property. These were some of the illegal activities I found out about immediately. I discovered more as time went by.

There was a Warrant Officer, W3 Morgan, assigned to the department who had been advanced to LTJG soon after my arrival. He informed me that the Criminal Investigation Division was about to install surveillance equipment on the time clocks. It had been reported fraud was committed routinely in the structural shops. When an employee had to work overtime, that person would punch the time cards for two or three others who never showed up for work. I questioned him about who had to sign or verify the accuracy of the time cards. His response was he didn't know but that probably no one showed up to check on them. I ask Morgan to request they allow me time to get things under control and the investigators agreed. I don't think they were eager to get involved with this bunch.

Most of the problems could be attributed to the supervision of the diversified work force by the military who didn't have the necessary training. In addition, time counted as shore duty for the officers who were stationed on the base, and was sea duty for the enlisted. This caused problems because many times enlisted and civilians had to take responsibilities which should have been on officer's shoulders. The prevailing attitude seemed to indicate everybody was laid back as if the time here was a vacation. I heard many times and from several different people, "when I get back to the real world" I will do so-and-so. A vivid example was offered by the civilian (WS 14) I replaced who was in court when I left Norfolk. He was a First Class Gunners Mate, who retired while stationed on the base, and was hired as a civilian to the position of Services Branch manager. He did something to get on the wrong side of a lawyer, who was a reserve officer, a Captain, on two weeks annual training. He took my predecessor to court for defrauding the government when he returned to the States and after the WS14 had retired. The man expanded a forty-two- thousand dollar job into eighty-two thousand by working overtime his last year before retiring. The judge reprimanded the witness, who had signed the man's overtime sheets, for his bad language on the witness stand. The Judge then dismissed the charges against the WS14. He admonished the reserve Captain Lawyer for bringing the wrong man before him. The judge correctly informed the lawyer the man using the bad language had the authority to grant or disapprove the overtime and he should be the one on trial. Overtime was required because the ships were in Gitmo for training and were only available for needed repairs on the weekends. They were out to sea doing training exercises during the week. The WS14 should have had the Chief checking the work and if he needed assistance, promote a non-US civilian to supervise the work in progress.

It was apparent by the problems I discovered the first few days that proper supervision was definitely lacking. I had a lot of work to do and I started by making a prioritized list and establishing goals. I considered the most important first step was to inform the troops what I expected of them, just as I had in the Navy. They were put on notice I was not going to allow the infractions that had occurred in the past. Using the Civilian Personnel Manual for guidance I made up a folder on each employee and held a brief one-on-one interview with each. I continued using these records to document infractions and the actions taken to correct. I informed each employee they could see their record at any time upon request. I ordered safety gear and insisted they wear steel tipped shoes at all times and hard hats when outside their shop on work sites. I demanded that they not overstay the guaranteed annual leave they were granted as had been customary in the past. I warned it could be grounds for termination if they did not return on time. The time clock and signing of time cards would be done correctly, and any discrepancies would be grounds for immediate termination. I also had to take a hard look at supervisory positions of which there were a definitely shortage. I didn't mind checking on the jobs being worked on the weekend but I was being paid much more than a non-US supervisor. I had no problem obtaining permission to advance deserving workers to foreman and leader positions once I determined who was qualified. It took time to evaluate their work and determine who were deserving and capable. I had to work several weekends to ensure all was as it should be, but only stayed a couple hours each time.

The hardest part of my job was firing employees who would not follow the guidelines established by the regulations. However, the termination of ten employees during the first year definitely gave the others a heads up.

The newly promoted foreman rigger was working on a tug in the dry dock for an overhaul one Saturday. The following Monday morning, he informed me a new hire was selling drugs to sailors from the engine room of the tugboat. I fired him immediately, and he followed me on my way to the BOQ after work. He ran me off the road, jumped out of his car and chased me around and around my car with a machete. I was lucky a couple cars stopped and a base police officer intervened, arrested and locked the idiot up at the police station. The man was detained until the next flight to the states, when he and his personal belongings were sent stateside permanently. During this time, the civilian personnel office called to ask me if I had located new jobs for contract employees that I had terminated. I said, why in the hell would I want to do that, if they were any good I would not have fired them. I was informed the State Department required a certain number of Jamaicans be maintained on our roles. I told her good luck at hiring replacements and please try to get some better ones this time. I don't know why but I never got along with that lady from then on.

Everything seemed to fall into place by the beginning of the second year. I was amazed that almost all of my employees had become outstanding workers. They seemed to take pride in their work as a team. My insistence that work assignments be distributed fairly to every employee worked wonders for morale. Infractions of the rules were a thing of the past with very few exceptions. I believe they realized I was not the enemy and that I was there to help by improving their working conditions, while at the same time improving production. I never stopped being amazed by the talent these Jamaicans and Cubans displayed. There was never a job turned away for lack of ability or talent and we took on some very difficult tasks in the three years I was at SRD. Whether it was in the dry dock or at a pier, I was convinced these men could do anything and do it well. The picture below is one of the jobs that required more than average skills.

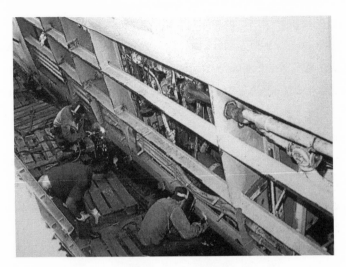

**All the stringers were replaced and ready
to install the hull plating.**

A large section of the hull plating had to be cropped out through a double row of rivets. I had no idea if any of them knew how to do riveting. There was also piping damage requiring repairs, in addition to the hull.

The Destroyer was sent to us for repairs to the large gash in her hull. She had hit a pier in the US Virgin Islands. The Shipfitters, Welders, Pipe Fitters and Riggers worked long hours to complete this job in a professional manner and in record time.

The Norfolk Naval Shipyard had x-rayed the welding, inspected the riveted joints and sent word back that everything passed.

There was another challenging job when an LPH came into port with two large patrol craft on board. They were scheduled for delivery to Jamaica so we were required to unload them. The problem was they were loaded in the center of the flight deck. Due to the height of the flight deck, my one-hundred ton crane would not reach that far inboard. Public Works had a portable ninety-ton crane, which I was allowed to use. By lifting and positioning it on the high deck with my crane, it could reposition the craft to the deck edge. However, the ship's captain was concerned that the localized weight on each wheel might damage his deck. After he placed a call to NAVSEA for advice, we were informed cribbing of a certain thickness should be used to distribute the weight just to be safe. We located enough lumber and situated it where the ninety-ton crane would be placed. I also had some boards placed to assist the crane in climbing the cribbing. We had a spreader bar and wire which we used to lift Jamaican patrol craft. We used these periodically when repairs were required and they also fit these boats. We used the floating crane to unload the repositioned craft, the wood cribbing and returned the portable crane to the pier.

I received a letter of appreciation for the ingenuity used in accomplishing the task. Everyone who participated received a letter of commendation from the CO for a job well done.

I was becoming uneasy about using the floating crane. On every lift, the old direct current switchboard arcing seemed to worsen. I went to CDR Edwards, who had relieved my former boss CDR Cooper, and attempted to discuss what I thought to be a safety issue with the crane. He did not want to talk about it. Therefore, I reduced my concerns to writing and submitted the letter to him with a copy to the Public Works Officer. During my research, I learned the Public Works Department had signature custody of the crane from the Corps of Army Engineers. After the PWO received my letter he notified me to place it out of commission and he would get back to me. As it turned out, NAVSEA had to be advised how long the crane would be out of service. They needed to know because it was the main battery for lifting anything in the Caribbean. The PWO took care of the necessary paper work and funding and the crane was towed to the States for a much needed overhaul.

I received word there was going to be a reduction in force (RIF) soon. Our Command was going to be transferred from the AIRLANT type Command to the SURVLANT Command. This would abolish all but one of the civilian positions including mine. I was prepared to exercise my return rights to my old position in the shipyard in Portsmouth even though I wasn't ready to leave.

Soon the day came when I was forced to make a decision about my future employment. I was offered the only civil service position available at SRD. It was a facilities manager at the GS11 grade and not a supervisory position. I would save pay at the present grade level regardless whether I stayed or returned to the States. There was an opening in the Public Works Department for a shop planner, WD6, I applied and was selected for the position.

They assigned me to the metal trades division as the tool room attendant issuing tools. It was an easy job and I had plenty of free time. This enabled me to read everything I could get my hands on about the functions of a Public Works Department. I didn't mind sitting on my posterior drawing twenty plus dollars an hour while preparing for advancement. After a few weeks of this, I was assigned to the supervisor of shop planners even though he was not functioning as the supervisor. He was located in building 688 where overflow stowage of material was stored. I still held an undefined job and continued my studies. After about three months had passed, I was tasked to write a report on how this department functioned compared to the books I was studying. The report was to evaluate how this PWD compared by listing the pros and cons as I viewed them. I learned later that this test was a standard procedure for all new officers checking into the department. I was fortunate a team from Naval Facilities Engineering Command from D.C. were onboard conducting a periodic inspection. My 12 page report was made available to them and word was that what I had submitted was ninety-five percent accurate.

I had been patient, but I could not tolerate remaining idle much longer. I started looking and applying for employment elsewhere. I applied for a GM13 position at the Long Beach Naval Shipyard as the welding shop superintendent. The employment office was advertising Nationwide because the position had been filled by advancing a man from the shop without advertising the position. The fear was the selection was open for a legitimate grievance, so they had to back up and start over. The general foreman in the shop got the position legally after all the interviewing was complete. I applied for a position in Guam and was notified that I had been selected when I returned to Gitmo.

Word reached the Public Works Officer, probably from personnel, of my selection and I was immediately promoted to a temporary GS12 position as the PWD Maintenance Manager. I was assigned to the Maintenance Control Director (MCD) who was an engineer GS12 and given a desk outside his glassed in office. I attempted to find out what my job was to entail by asking the assistant Public Works Officer and others. The answer I received in response was "that office needs a lot of help". After examining the files I knew where I needed to start. I requested and was given two full time secretaries for typing. I removed the large Plexiglas status boards, which covered one wall beside my desk. I replaced the status board of job orders with a typed list for distribution to all who required the information. I included in the report for distribution, the date received and the status of material required. It was amazing the length of time many of these had been in the filing cabinets. After investigating, I found the reason to be lack of material, even though material had been received, but unaccounted for in the staging area. A decision the PWO must make was how to handle the jobs from resident commands. Without the material, the jobs would never be accomplished. The choices were, order the missing material and pay for it out of Public Works funds, or cancel the job orders and send the requests back. The decision was to send them back, so my secretaries pulled the job orders from the list I had provided, and returned them. The next evolution was more time consuming. I had a couple men, using a five-ton truck, load the material that was still there which had been purchased for these jobs. This material was relocated to Bldg. 688 for stowage with all other excess material. The material from the staging area was inventoried and marked with the name of the Command that had paid for it.

Unknown to me, the PWO had been attempting to get permission for a GM13 position in order to hire a Superintendent for several months. After receiving approval, the position was advertised locally. There were three applicants for the job. A WS13, two GS12's, one was an engineer, the other a retired naval officer. We were interviewed and considered for the job and I was selected. My selection did not sit well with the others, who thought they were more qualified than I. My proven record demonstrating my ability to improve production in more than one Command and in more than one position was the reason I was selected.

The obvious problem with production was, once again, lack of hands on supervision. The kind of supervision accomplished down in the trenches, not from an office sitting behind a desk. I knew exactly what needed to be changed the day I turned in the PWD report. I had knowledge of the methods to improve production, and the type supervision that was required to accomplish the desired results.

In a PW Department the shops engineer is normally the supervisor of all shops and production. In a Public Works Center, a superintendent has those responsibilities. We worked out a reasonable working arrangement between the LCDR, who was the shops engineer and me. He and I discussed it several times. We did not know if we were to work alongside each other, or if I was to be his replacement. Officers supervised some of our five divisions and there were several enlisted Sea Bees among the five hundred employees in those divisions. We decided he would take care of all military matters, and I would be free to concentrate on production. We discussed our decision with the Assistant Public Officer and approval was granted. The PWO, APWO, Shops Engineer and a few others had call letters followed by a number. I heard some joking around about what call letter to assign me. The call sign Z1 was discussed because then I would represent "Zorro", the sword-banishing hero from the movies. I knew then what was expected of me as Superintendent. I'm surprised I wasn't issued a sword. I don't remember what call letter I ended up with, but I had a couple two way radio's in the jeep which was assigned to me. That jeep was where I spent the majority of my working hours until I departed Gitmo.

I was offered an office within the PWD administration building, where all managers, including the Shops Engineer were located. I declined, and instead, went to each shop and selected what I thought to be the best location for my office. This happened to be the office of the General Foreman for the building trades. I requested he allow me to move to his office and he find another. He didn't seem to mind, in fact, he was more than willing, and even helped me move. A very bright young civilian lady was assigned to assist in the office. I saw her a few years later when she was working at the Naval Station Mayport as the CO's secretary.

It was about this time I received a letter from the Department of the Navy inviting me to return to active duty. There was a shortage in the present ranks of active duty personnel who were familiar with the compartment numbering' firefighting systems and other antiquated systems I was one of several receiving letters to teach these assets to the crew of the Battle Wagon being placed back into service. It was about a week before I had enough nerve to open my mail again.

The bottleneck in production was for the most part, with material and assignment of work. The logistics of obtaining all material from the states to an isolated Naval Base in a communist country could be a problem. The bigger problem was not ordering or receiving the required material, it was how it was used when it arrived. There was a lot of robbing "Peter to pay Paul" going on. The second major problem was work assignments caused by the absence of a formal or systematic method of scheduling. To further delay production, shop supervisors would assign a crew to work a job on Monday morning only to find out all the material needed for the job was not there. This situation would not exist had they utilized the shop planners whose job is to verify the material status before men are assigned. This is more than likely one reason material was being taken from other jobs. Another reason for the pilfering of material was managers ordering jobs started without knowledge of material availability Now that the problems were identified, we could go forward with solutions. I had the disseminated listing of job orders pending, broken down by material on order and material complete. One full time employee was required to insure the list was maintained current in MCD. I convinced everyone who received this list, that only jobs with all the material complete could be placed on the work schedule. A Stateside hire, to be the full time scheduler, was brought on board with this job as his primary duty. The shop planners were assigned to the shops, and used as they should have been all along. They were to locate and verify all material for jobs scheduled for the following week was on hand and available. The Planners and Estimators who received the approved work orders were required to search the excess material in building 688 prior to ordering any material. By doing this for every job order, it reduced the vast amount of excess material on hand which had been inventoried and separated.

Centralized scheduling also provided a contact for managers or anyone who had a preference as to when a job would be started.

Shops could not assign work without a supporting job order and not then if it was not on the schedule. If the shops had extra man-hours to utilize, the supervisors would go to scheduling for additional work assignments. I held weekly production meetings to listen to problems and if possible, prevent or correct hard spots. One problem area, that was identified, was how to handle the scheduling when multiple trades were required on a job. I decided we would handle it the same way as the shipyard. The trade, which was in support of the lead shop, would make that job their priority. This would insure there would be no delays or dead time due to lack of man power on any job in progress. Once everyone was on board with the new scheduling effort production increased drastically. It was not only noticeable, but also measurable by the number of job orders being accomplished compared to before. Now I had time to go to job sites with work in progress, check and help with existing problems first hand.

I was divorced from my first wife, while working in the Ship Repair Department. I married my second wife, Carol, about the same time I started to work at Public Works. I moved from the BOQ to senior officers housing at Iguana Circle. We lived in a four bedroom, two-bath house overlooking the golf course. Her daughter and mine spent their summers with us. They had a great time swimming and horseback riding. Carol had cancer that was in remission, but unfortunately, it raised its ugly head again a few months before I had five years overseas. Since she could not get treatment on base, we returned to the States, and I was placed on leave without pay and remained in that status for three months. I called at the end of three months after it was determined she would most likely be fighting a long battle. It was very good of the Public Works Officer, Captain Lou Fermo, to keep my position open, but it was now a situation with an unpredictable outcome.

The Captain, unlike many others, he came to Gitmo to do a job, and he worked hard at that job. The many improvements he made to the base, and accomplishments he achieved by his organizing efforts as the PWO was amazing There were lots of jokes about his "green grams" we would find on our desks on Monday mornings. The notes pertained mostly to work required in the area of the recipient's responsibility. He toured the base every weekend looking for deficiencies that needed correcting. I never heard anyone complain about the notes, penned in green ink, in a cruel manner. We all knew they served to get work accomplished that would otherwise go unnoticed. When it came to hard work he led by example. We have kept in touch over the years and I have enjoyed the many emails and holiday messages from him.

I placed a call to the APWO to inform him of my decision to terminate and return long enough to pack out my house hold belongings and move back to Virginia Beach. I used the Public Works Officers phone at the Amphibious Base to keep in touch with Gitmo. He had been the APWO when I was first employed in the Public works Department in Cuba. In fact, he was the one requesting I submit the twelve page report on the PWD operation.

It was in October 1984 when she lost her battle with cancer.

I exercised my return rights to my old job in the Progress Section of the shipyard with save pay at the GM13 level in October 1984.

I was led to my old familiar desk by Willie who was the supervisor and I found the same three pennies I had left in the drawer. I was getting my personal items stashed away when he brought a young lady by for me to meet. I already knew all the others, she was the only new employee hired since I depart almost five years before. She was a very pretty girl so after we were introduced I said the Progress Section workers are getting a lot prettier. He came back to my desk later and warned me against saying things like that to women. I responded, is it OK if I say the old bastards in here are uglier than ever? Apparently, the shipyard had experienced some sexual harassment complaints but I hardly think a compliment would fall into that category. I had recommended the welding shop supervisor, Jay Rhue from FMAG to take my job. I knew he would do a good job because he was a very hard worker.

I asked Willie about him and he said they had hired him off the water front as a welder. Not long after he was hired, a job came open with the Supervisor of Ship Building which he applied for and was awarded the position.

I was assigned to the USS Forestall to follow the progress of the overhaul of the magazine spaces. It was not a challenging job and it would have lasted for several months, had I remained employed.

The PWD Budget and Administration Officer from Cuba, Lillian Partlow, had been informed by a friend that Carol had passed away. Both she and her friend were back in the real world. Her friend was in D.C and Lillian was employed in the same position she left when she took a job overseas. She was Fleet Training Center Budget/ Supply Officer, Mayport Naval Station FL where she retired. I received a card and an invitation to visit, and attend the Gator Bowl football game. We were joined at the game by her Aunt, brother and friend. I didn't know Lil very well, just that we both attended the Captain's weekly meeting every Wednesday. I did know she was an attractive lady, easy to talk to and I admired her work ethics, she was a very hard worker. I accepted the invitation, and she met me at the airport in her navy blue T-Bird with a jug of Bloody Marys. As we left the airport, she asked me to pour us one, and I asked her if she wanted to go to jail. She informed me it was legal to have a drink while driving. I knew in Virginia you could get your car impounded and you would go to jail if caught drinking and driving. I spent a week at her home in Neptune Beach. We talked a lot and walked on the beach. and on Christmas day it was eighty degrees!

When I returned to work I went to the glass enclosure and ask the boss, Mr. Youngblood, how long would it take to quit this job? He said he didn't know because no one had ever quit. I went to the personnel office and learned it would take about three days. I returned to his office and informed him I would be leaving at the end of the week. He requested that I write a "lessons learned" report for continuity to assist the person who would be assigned to my job. I finished the report, was tested for asbestoses exposure, and completed the checkout. Mr. Youngblood gave a presentation, an award with a plaque, and informed the other employees I was going to Florida for another job. Why he said that, I don't know, because he knew I was retiring, but he must have had a reason.

I took a couple of days off, then packed a few belongings and headed south. I had made the decision to relocate to the sunshine State and started looking for a house soon after arriving. I found a house Lil and I both liked, so I bought it and made arrangements for my household goods to be delivered

Lil and I hung out together, got to know each other well enough to get married on April 5th, 1986 after I had been living in Neptune Beach for sixteen months.

She moved to my house and we rented her's for a year before placing it on the market for sale. Lil wanted to sell her house after we married but I didn't, for two reasons. First, I knew I would be selling my properties in Virginia and it would add to our tax burden. The second reason was plain common sense; she might decide to go home after that first year. We made several trips to my place in VA Beach to check on the three properties I owned. On the last trip, we decided to place all three on the market for sale.

I didn't know what I wanted to do with my time so I decided to get a real estate license. I took a crash course, passed the test and received a salesman's license. I didn't really want to get into that grind again. I was financially able to retire and that was my intention. Although I didn't take selling real estate seriously, I did sell a couple houses.

An opportunity to appraise real estate presented itself, this interested me, and so I did that for about eight months. I soon tired of the aggravation of working and quit. I found out being a beach bum was a lot more fun. I became a professional at walking or riding my bike on the beach and doing nothing. Even that was boring after a while, so I started landscaping the yard, had a pool installed and a yard sprinkler system. A friend helped me build a five-hundred square foot shop. I completed it by locating the sprinkler and pool pumps inside the shop and making a driveway to the street. A few years later, I helped him build a mountain retreat in North Carolina.

I had an acquaintance from Gitmo who had returned to PWD Mayport to his former job as the Maintenance Control Director. He came to the house one afternoon to discuss a new program they wanted to establish at Mayport. This program would be a Long Range Maintenance Plan for on base facilities. After he explained all the details, I accepted the offer to head up the LRMP. I agreed to give the project one year but completed or not I would be leaving. I had been retired for several years, and I enjoyed working with wood in the garage and later in the shop I built in the back yard. The personnel office called and offered me the job at the entry step of a GS11. I told the lady I was a GM13 when I quit so bump that offer to the top step and I would take the position. She informed me she would have to call me back, which she did, and I accepted the offer of the top step. What intrigued me about the position, was not supervising six experienced Planner-Estimators, but that all their work would be computerized then put into a central data bank. There were no programs of this kind in existence at the time which could be used as a guide. I was given priority for the services of a programmer already onboard. The programmer established the computerized programs I would need to start while I was selected employees to fill my small work force. Two of my estimators and I attended two weeks of training at the Public Works Center, NOB in Norfolk. This facility had the information I would need. The LRMP was primarily designed to estimate work required on facilities and place a print ready job order in the data bank. The job orders would be prioritized by importance and scheduled for accomplishment based on necessity. As an example, we would no longer paint buildings when the roof was leaking. We also inventoried the equipment which would require periodic maintenance or replacement in each facility. I found weekly training was necessary to keep everyone on track and working the same routine. I kept a close watch on the information which went into the central data base. It was also important to take notes that I could use to write an instruction and operations manual once all the details were worked out. After we were in full operation, the Public Works Officer requested I brief the base Captain on the program. During the first few minutes of the briefing he commented; "nobody is going to tell me how I'm going to spend my money". This ended my presentation. His attitude was unfortunate, but it did not have a negative effect on our mission, which was to make LRMP the new standard for facility management.

Accurate estimates and necessary reports would determine the failure or success of the program. It was proven successful by the end of the first year. We were able to print and issue prepared work orders covering nearly half million dollars in "dump" money in one day. Dump money is funding given from other commands that are unable to obligate it by the end of the year. No command wants to return funding for fear of losing the same amount in the following year's budget. The beauty of being able to issue the work orders quickly was the fact that all high priority work was identified so the funding would be used wisely.

I was ready to resign because I felt the program was established and proven successful. Before I could finish the letter of resignation, I received a request from the PWO. He asked me to take on the duties of the Operations-Maintenance (O&M) contractor who had just defaulted on his contract. I agreed, and was promoted to GS12, relieved of all other duties and started to work as the PWD superintendent. The contractor left eighty-five employees on base, many of who had not been paid. I learned he had used the material he was provided for shop supplies. He also left the vehicles in need of servicing, maintenance and repairs. There was not a roll of toilet paper or a paper towel in any of his assigned spaces. Supplies for water, sewage and boiler treatment to enable the continuation of services was in critical short supply.

I gathered all the employees together and informed them what I planned to do. I told the employees they would become temporary government employees. Any person who didn't want to do this could feel free to leave. Everybody opted to stay, so I gathered the pertinent information and went to the civilian personnel office to assist them in the hiring process. The employment phase took the better part of one day. I started interviewing them one at a time to insure there was sufficient supervision and found there was critical shortages in all the trades. The General foreman was in place, but it was obvious the contractor had been saving money by not having first line supervisors where needed. I augmented with men from the public works department to fill in as temporary foremen in their field of expertise. I also filled in with personnel qualified to do open purchase ordering which I knew was going to be needed if we were to maintain critical services without outages. We needed supplies for work and money to pay outside firms he had rented machinery from such as sewage lift pumps. Apparently he didn't have qualified personnel to repair the pumps in place. I discovered a severe shortage of qualified personnel required for the three shifts necessary in the boiler plant. It was important to provide steam for the ships in cold iron status as well as the base. It was necessary to hire additional temporary employees there. For the other shortages, we were able to fill by reassigning the talent we already had.

I also had a representative from the Department of Labor meet with the employees who had not been paid. However, all she could do was go after the contractor who owed them the wages. The supervisor in charge of the water treatment plant came to me concerned that he had men who couldn't leave home because they couldn't pay for child care. There were others who didn't even have money to buy gas to get to work. I told the foreman I could not hand out money to individuals but if he would be responsible for repaying the money I would loan him enough to keep the water plant manned. He came back with a request for six hundred dollars and I gave it to him before quitting time. I had two men who had open purchase authority working diligently gathering supplies requested by the foremen I had assigned from in house. Those supplies were critical in order to maintain services to places such as base housing, and to keep pier services, the boiler plant, water treatment, sewage and electrical working without disruption. We just did not have the luxury of time to go through the proper supply channels.

Before long the Supply Officer who was responsible for keeping open purchasing to a minimum complained to the Captain about our excessive abuses. I had to meet with the base XO, PWO and the supply Officer who had a list of specific items we had purchased without going through his department. One by one the Supply Officer would read my violation and the PWO would say, Strode can you fix that, and I would say yes to every complaint. Everyone at that table knew the number one objective was to keep the base functioning, utilities operable and that I was going to achieve that, regardless of the Supply Department rules.

We had accomplished the transition from contractor to in house operations without a single outage and for the most part using temporary employees. I had to report back to the base a few times when it became necessary to call workers in for emergencies but that was to be expected. I was pleased by the fact I never had a problem getting the men to respond when called

The PWO asked me to prepare a contingency plan for submittal to NAVFAC because he had seen most of the necessary documents I had prepared. I had already made work flow chart, personnel requirements for each trade, and organizational charts. We even established a trouble desk for emergency work requests. There were additional documents necessary to facilitate our take over to insure a smooth transition. I put it in sequential format, and included a few extra details to complete a comprehensive overview of the job we were doing. I learned later that this plan was accepted by NAVFAC without change. In the future, it was to be used by any Public Works Departments who experienced contractor default as Mayport had.

I was asked to review the specifications contained in the new contract, which was being prepared to go out for bids. I was required to sit on the evaluation board during the interviews. A short time after the interviews were completed, a contractor was onboard. I met with the contractor to discuss the employee situation. I began by informing the new O&M contractor that he would find all systems and equipment in excellent working condition. This was due to the exceptional performance and team work by the workers who had been left unemployed by the former contractor. With few exceptions, I advised him he should hire them to continue in their current positions. I informed him who I believed would make good supervisors to replace the PWD employees I had used if required.

I had a current inventory of the materials on hand, which had been purchased, that were necessary for use on a daily basis. Decisions had to be made on how the turn-over would be handled and other matters requiring the attention of my superiors.

I had been repaid the six hundred dollars I loaned the water treatment plant foreman. The loan was mentioned in the full page letter of appreciation I received from the Commanding Officer.

I turned in my resignation in March 1990 and returned to retirement where I have remained for the past twenty four years.

15280230R00137

Made in the USA
Middletown, DE
02 November 2014